TABLE OF CONTENTS

Preface (JUST READ IT, IT'S SHORT)

CAUTION: If you are a professional editor, a self-proclaimed grammar queen, or if you are reading American literature in the hopes of improving your English, READ NO FURTHER! This book is full of (mostly intentional) grammatical errors, goofy punctuation, and colloquialisms (hey, I spelled that right on the first try!). This is NOT a book for the grammatically faint-hearted!

I have to make a couple of disclaimers. This book may contain errors. Well, it probably *does* have errors. Maybe lots of them. The reason being, this book is dealing with good ol' boys and they "just don' talk rite," so I couldn't very well send this to an editor, because most editors have OCD and the style with which I wrote this book would make any self-respecting bibliophile (that's *book lover* for us regular folk) twitch with uncontrollable spasms. Seriously. So, if you're looking for an example of literary genius, you might want to move on to the Charles Dickens section. Just a suggestion.

Now, because we're dealing with good ol' boys who are common sense challenged and grew up watching Evel Knievel perform jaw-dropping gravity-defying stunts, I have to make the standard cover-our-butts-so-we-don't-get-sued statement. You know, the statement they have to make at the beginning of that certain show (now made into movies…seriously?) with the guys who perform such spectacular stunts as attaching battery cables to their testicles or forcing one another to eat earthworms that have spent three months fermenting in human sewage. What a bunch of jackasses. Yeah. That show. This book is *nothing* like that, mind you, although there are some pretty asinine stunts perpetrated by our boys here. Needless to say, *DON'T TRY THIS AT HOME*. Our boys were semi-professionals (well, they were all working for a living anyway) when they performed these feats of stupidity, and they did take safety precautions (sort of…I mean, holding your friend's beer does prevent spillage and keeps him from knocking himself in the head with the bottle upon landing), so don't think you and Billy Ray Bob are going to live through launching a school bus over a stack of cars just because our main dude managed to survive such a feat (after much time in the hospital, mind you).

Also, since the stories are sorta-kinda mostly true (aside from the typical "my fish was bigger" embellishment that goes on with such things), the names and places have been changed to protect the inno…well, to protect da boyz from embarrassment now that they're "all growed up" and are trying to act like respectable adults in their middle-aged years (the real reason for the acting responsible is because most of them are pretty broken up and wired together with more hardware than Steve Austin—that's the Six Million Dollar Man for you youngsters, Google it. Otherwise, they would probably *still* be acting like donkeys' behinds). Changing stuff might possibly even protect them from lawsuits once Ol' Lady Crawford finds out just who it was who rained glow sticks down in her front yard and decorated her house, cars, dogs, cat, livestock, et cetera, with paintballs.

Our fearless leader and main character wanted his name to be "Rock," because, well, he thinks The Rock is cool. He even said, "When they make this into a movie, I want The Rock to play me, okay?" Sure, buddy. Whatever you say. Never mind that he looks nothing like Dwayne Johnson. Oh, he's a big guy like Dwayne, but he has a long ponytail down his back and is as white as Rock's sheep used to be before the paintball incident (which you shall read about later). But assuming this little old book would ever be made into a movie is a bit farfetched. I mean, seriously, just trying to find stuntmen willing to do the crazy stunts da boyz pulled off and somehow survived would be pretty much impossible.

I also cleaned up the language a bit to make this more of a PG rated version. Well, maybe PG-13. But since we are dealing with those types of boy-men who have the construction-worker type mentality, there are going to be some colorful words that even I, your fearful yet faithful author, can't fix. So, fair-warning. Get your Sunday School filter glasses out if you are of a delicate constitution. Or, better yet, move on to that Charles Dickens section. Insert winky face here.

Oh, one other thing—the stories aren't in chronological order (that's date order for those of you who don't do much reading past the cable TV guide), so don't get too confused when you go from a pre-teen Rock to adult Rock and back again. Honestly, there isn't much difference between the two, other than a beer gut.

Alrighty then, I do believe that covers our disclaimer slash preface section, so let us move on to …

Chapter 1 FINDING OUT GRAVITY SUCKS

Cars, Bikes and Boobs

There comes a time in every future stuntman's life when he discovers gravity. And the fact that gravity is a real bummer. But if it weren't for that nasty law of physics that Sir Isaac Newton so rudely discovered, *everyone* would have the capability of performing amazing death-defying feats, and then said feats wouldn't be so amazing. Or death-defying. So apparently there is a good use for gravity, besides keeping us from floating off into space.

Rock's story begins at age eleven, when he first came to the realization that gravity does, in fact, suck. He wasn't yet old enough to appreciate the planet-grounding effect of that particular law, and so anything that had the potential of keeping him from flying was not on his list of favorite things.

He also wasn't alone in his flying fantasies. Rock had managed to surround himself with a whole pack of like-minded goombas. The wannabe stuntmen, aka boyz in da 'hood, were always up to the gravity-defying challenge of jumping something with their bikes, like stacks of wood, trash cans, Mrs. Thompson's cat (that was quite a feat, since the cat flat-out refused to cooperate), and other assorted junk.

They had pretty much run out of cool things to jump and were discussing the dilemma one day. That's when KC said something along the lines of "Too bad we can't jump a car."

Rock immediately responded with, "Why not?" KC then proceeded to give him all the reasons why not, the foremost being that it was too crazy.

Oooooh, a challenge. Any self-respecting male couldn't back down from that. So "challenge accepted" it was.

"Here, hold my RC." (The boys weren't old enough to drink beer, obviously. Duh.)

Rock's mom had a'68 Ford Galaxy. Those were the days when cars were made of actual metal and could engage in minor fender benders without having to call the insurance company and an ambulance chasing attorney. Not like the plastic cars nowadays, where you tap the guy in front of you at one mile an hour and end up with a thousand dollar estimate to replace your entire grill because the plastic pieces shattered like an Easter egg. No, cars in those days could take a hit. Heck, even a small meteorite falling at a bazillion miles an hour wouldn't do more than scratch the paint. It was like driving a Panzer tank. Or maybe a land submarine. Yeah, those were the days.

Moving on. So Rock decided to test his prepubescent theory that one eleven-year-old on an aluminum frame Husky bicycle could, in fact, make it over a car approximately the length of a USS Franklin D. Roosevelt, using just a piece of wood, a little speed and a large set of…well, you know—those external dangly bits of anatomy that produce a hormone which gives the male species the misguided idea that they are immortal.

This lack of planning and abundance of prepubescent testosterone would have benefitted from an advanced physics lesson. And a landing ramp. Not to mention a helmet. And paramedics on stand-by.

Once the board was properly laid against the trunk of the car that was shining oh-so-brightly thanks to the barely-a-week-old pearl white paint job Rock's mom had wanted so badly and saved for months to get, Rock headed up a small hill behind the house with his bike. He assumed the small slope would provide enough down grade for his body weight plus the total gross vehicle weight of the bike to propel at the proper amount of speed to clear the car. Well, okay, Rock of course didn't think like that, being that he was only eleven and hormonally brain cell challenged. But he did figure the hill would help him get the speed he needed to fly over the car. Or at least he hoped.

Let's put ourselves in mini Rock's place here for a minute. So here we are at the top of the little hill, looking down at that pretty, sparkling white paint job with the board haphazardly propped against the trunk, our little heart a-pounding at the prospect of being the next Evel Knievel, hoping beyond hope that some talent scout will hear of our amazing feat of bravery and our complete and utter lack of common sense and come knocking on our door, begging our parents to move to Hollywood so we can be the next Super Stuntman in all the blockbuster movies and our friends will be so envious that they'll turn practically Kermit the Frog green.

Da boyz were whooping and hollering and Rock knew he couldn't stall any longer. It was now or never. Never was looking pretty good at that point, especially when he realized that, if by some unforeseen event (like maybe the hill wasn't as high as he thought and he couldn't get enough speed, or maybe a bird might swoop down right at the moment he was about to hit the ramp and knock him off course, or a big gust of wind might come up at the last minute and blow him over into the neighbor's yard).

KC cupped his hands around his mouth and yelled, "Go!" Procrastination time was over. *Dang it.*

Back in Rock's shoes, we're now pedaling as fast as we can, we take off down the little hill, sure that we're nearing Mach I. Or maybe even Warp 2. About to break the sound barrier, anyway. Our eyes are glued to that piece of wood that's supposed to be our launch pad, concentrating hard on that little strip of wood so we don't miss it. That would be bad. Like really, *really* bad.

We're now realizing as we get closer and closer to our target that this probably wasn't the best idea we've ever had, that we maybe shoulda coulda woulda thought this through a little more, made a better plan, a better design for a launch ramp. But we're committed now. No backing out now, not unless we want to look like a puss…uh, a wimp.

So, eyes on what now seems to be our death sentence in a two-inch wide piece of wood, we see the few short years of our life passing before our now suddenly misty eyes. *No!* We yell at our self. *No self-respecting stuntman cries, for Pete's sake!*

To calm down, we begin an internal dialog. *Okay, I'm not crying. My eyes are just burning from doing near light speed with no goggles. I should have thought about that. Next time I'll have to dig through my toy box and find those swimming goggles Mom bought for me last summer when the chlorine at the pool was messing up my eyes. But I think those things had a Superman S in the middle, didn't they? I'm way too old for Superman. I mean, seriously, I'm practically a man now. I can't be wearing Superman stuff. That's not cool at all. I wonder if that make Speed Racer goggles…*

And with that last thought, we realize we've arrived at our destination. *Oh, crap! Here we go! I hope Mom won't be too mad if I die…*

The front tire hits the bottom of the ramp and our teeth rattle as our direction suddenly changes when we're propelled upward on the board that now seems about as wide as a toothpick split in half. Our already impossibly tight grip on the handlebars squeezes even tighter, like a gargantuan boa constrictor choking the life out of its victim Our fingers dig so hard into the rubber handgrips that we can feel the cold metal underneath.

The bike has now become a NASA rocket, just like those we've seen on television, the kind that can launch all the way to the moon. Our mind wanders once again, as we wonder if we can, in fact, make it to the moon ourselves. *We would probably have to build a sort of shell to cover the bike to keep meteors and space junk and stuff from beating us to death. That could be the next ultra-cool project.*

But then we force our mind to concentrate on the current stunt, which is starting to make us seriously reconsider what is kind of looking like a less-than-stellar idea, as we have now hit the end of the board and are flying free.

Whoa, we're really high! We can see the top of our house. *Hey! There's where my Nerf ball went!* We can see over the top of the neighbor's eight foot wall and into their backyard—*I didn't know they had a pool! Cool! We'll have to sneak in there tonight and go skinny dipping.* We can see across the street to where Tom's sister is helping her mother plant rosebushes in the garden, wearing only a blue and green striped bikini. *Wow, I never noticed she had boobs before!*

We are now looking at the top of the car and the hood as we continue to fly through space and realize that we have flipped upside down. At first we worry, wondering if we'll be able to flip back around before hitting the ground... *Oh, crap! I didn't think about a landing ramp! This is gonna hurt...*

It did.

Rock made it over the trunk of the freshly painted pearly white'68 Galaxy, and it was no small miracle that he'd managed to keep his tires centered on the toothpick-sized launch pad. He even succeeded in clearing the top of the car after hitting the end of the board. Amazingly, he actually made it over the hood of the car, even while doing a totally cool unintentional flip. Clearing the big, shiny steel bumper, however, is another story.

When gravity took hold and ruined Rock's amazing death-defying stunt, his front tire clipped the bumper of his Mom's car and sent him spiraling, causing KC to later proclaim as he stared down at Rock who was sprawled on the ground like a ripped up rag doll, "That was the coolest flip ever, man! You looked like one of those fireworks you nail to the fence that spin around all crazy. You gotta do that again!"

This is where that saying "With friends like these, who needs enemies?" came from. Well, maybe. It's possible anyway.

Results: One broken collarbone and his first concussion.

Shells and Bells

There was a time when all boys wanted to be great hunters, enthralled with weapons of all sorts, and camping was the best adventure they could ever imagine. Back when men could act the way they were created to, full of fight and might and boogers. This was back in the days before society decided manly men were knuckle-dragging Neanderthals who needed cultural refinement and a heavy dose of metrosexualism in order to be deemed acceptable by the general population.

This was when, at the scary age of twelve, after he had healed from his car-jumping injuries the summer before and had gotten off of an inhumanely long lock-down (also known as "grounding"), Rock and company decided it would be real fun and intelligent to shoot birds. In the neighborhood. On a Saturday. When everyone was home. And outside doing yard work.

Yeah.

Knowing they would all be beaten to within an inch of their life (yep, back then parents could actually discipline their kids without fear of the SWAT team showing up) if they even thought of touching a firearm, the ingenious little stinkers decided they would find a piece of wood that had a knot hole just the right size for a shotgun shell. Then all they would have to do would be to prop the board up, aim it at the sky and the unsuspecting blackbirds, and whack the end of the shell to shoot it off.

It took awhile, but the prepubescent geniuses finally found a board that wasn't termite-ridden or rotting and that had a knot hole just the right size for a shell (probably the same board they had used the year before for the now infamous'68 Galaxy jump). It was a good board.

Now the boys were just smart enough to know they couldn't whack the end of the shell with just any ol' thing. It had to be something heavy. Preferably metal. Like a hammer.

Setting the board up so the knot hole was aimed at the telephone wire that was sagging from the weight of all those fat blackbirds—which started an argument about whether or not blackbirds were, in fact, good eating, or even remotely edible—the boys piled rocks around the bottom to stabilize the weapon of mass destruction and set off to find a big hammer.

Let's get a mental image of this: the overly long board is propped up with a small pile of rocks, angled just right so the knot hole is aimed directly at the telephone wire where all those juicy, fat blackbirds have parked their feathered butts, looking all snotty and superior like "you can't touch me cuz I can *fly*", mocking the boys with their beady, weird little eyes; the shotgun shell is poked into the knot hole and Rock has a big-for-a-twelve-year-old hammer grasped between his two sweaty hands, cocked back and ready to shoot as he stands directly behind the board. (If you have any knowledge and/or experience with ballistics, you can see what's coming, can't you?)

KC counts off. "Five, four, three, two, ONE!" Rock, heart pounding and eyes squeezed shut, swings the hammer and manages a direct hit, right onto the gunpowder end of the shell.

BOOM!

It worked! The noise was deafening and the boys had to shake their heads to clear them.

But sadly, Rock never did see whether any snotty and superior birds suffered an untimely death that day, because when he struck the shotgun shell with the hammer and it exploded as they're designed to do, it created such a kickback that the board slammed back and hit Rock square between the eyes.

Results: One broken nose; concussion numero dos.

Jungle Gym

As did boys who were lucky enough to have television in their homes back in that day, Rock grew up watching Ron Ely as Tarzan The Ape Man. Yeah, that crazy dude who beat his chest like a gorilla and swung through the trees on amazingly strong vines that hung from branches in suspiciously spaced-just-right locations, which allowed the slightly savage, overly-muscular man easy access through the jungle with more efficiency than an Amazonian Greyhound bus.

Growing up in a neighborhood near a river, the trees grew to immense proportions, at least to a young man's eyes. This, coupled with too much time watching television on Saturday morning, meant someone came up with the less-than-bright idea of tying ropes high up in the trees so that they could copy the bulging ape man. Girls would surely think that was cool, right? By this age, the boys were starting to think of ways to impress the young ladies of the neighborhood, especially Tom's sister and her fantastic boobs, and hopefully soaring through trees at light speeds several stories above the hard ground would do the trick. Thankfully, though, the boys decided to skip the loincloths.

Having begun to learn the painful lesson that whenever a particularly dangerous stunt was performed, safety measures should be taken, the boys looked at the proposed stunt from different angles. Of course, they were only in the beginning stages of understanding pain and death and hadn't quite grasped the concept of safety equipment just yet.

The incredibly thought-out safety measure for this particular stunt was making sure the ropes were good—well, at least they weren't too old, anyway. They didn't look frayed. Yep, they should be strong enough to swing a couple of ninety-pound, Tarzan-bellowing, slightly-insane, barely-teenage males through the swaying cottonwoods. Hopefully.

After spacing the ropes far enough apart to ensure a good swing arc, the boys stood underneath the trees, looking up at their handiwork. Sure that their efforts would have impressed the Tarzan set designers in Hollywood, they decided Rock should be the first to take the trial run...or, swing, rather. Or "Totally Cool Death Plunge," as the stunt later came to be known.

Rock tied a string around the bottom of the first rope to be used in the Totally Cool Death Plunge and attached the other end to his belt loop, and then back up the tree our fearless—aka *brainless*—hero *cough "dork" cough*—went, climbing up, up, up, nearly to the top of the first cottonwood in a long line of the huge trees.

Snagging his swinging rope several times on branches on the way up, Rock was wondering if Mother Nature might be trying to stop him from something maybe he shouldn't be doing. He shook that thought off, however, instead reminding himself once again of the soon-to-be-had fame he was sure to get when word of his latest stunt reached Hollywood, just knowing that *this* time those producers would be begging him to come be the latest, greatest, death-defying stuntman.

Rock clung to the trunk of the tree while balancing on an inch-wide branch and untied the string from his belt loop before grabbing the rope by the foot-hold knot he'd tied in it. He took a moment to survey his surroundings, noticing that he seemed to be a bit higher now than when they had climbed the trees to tie the ropes. The distance between the trees and each swinging rope seemed a lot farther too. He almost had to squint to see the next rope he was supposed to grab on his swing. It seemed so very far away, hanging in yonder tree.

As he looked at yonder tree, his eyes rounded a bit when he realized it really was pretty danged far to said yonder tree from where he was perched in that cottonwood like a twitching squirrel who'd just discovered a stash of chocolate covered coffee beans. Yonder tree's trunk looked pretty large, too —and hard. And the next rope was dangling from a branch right in front of that trunk.

Rock was suddenly reminded of the George of the Jungle cartoon he had seen just last Saturday morning and winced when he remembered the way George slammed into a banana tree whilst attempting to swing through the jungle. And, cartoon or not, George was an expert tree swinger. Maybe there was something to be said for growing up in the jungle and learning the ropes. Rock snickered to himself at his joke.

But now was not the time for wimping out. The guys were down below —way, way, *way* down below—and were looking up at him, hollering their encouragements along the lines of "You wuss! Quit stalling!" and "Rock is a big chicken...bawwwwwk bawwwwk!" He couldn't back down now, or else they'd never let him live it down. But then, at least he'd *live*...

Shaking those gloomy thoughts off and gathering his nuts, Rock decided that if he missed the second rope and ended up slamming into yonder tree, he could just hope that he left a Rock-shaped imprint in the trunk. That would be so cool. Painful, but cool.

Trying to ignore the taunts from his unsupportive friends, Rock took a few deep breaths and found himself once again questioning the planning of this particular stunt, questioning his decision to go first, questioning whether he was too old to cry for his mommy.

But, no, Rock was a man, dang it, and no *real* man would ask his mother to get him out of a dangerous situation, even if it were one he had gotten into himself, with a little help from his friends. No, a real man would take the bull by the horns, go for the brass ring, stare danger in the eye and declare "I ain't skeered of nothin'!" and just go for it. So he did.

After one last "baaaawk baaaawk" from KC and a misguided "gobble gobble" from Tom that got him punched in the arm and called "stupid" by Ray, Rock took yet another deep breath and leapt. Well, it was more like a fall, because he'd lost his balance. But he wasn't going to admit that. Ever.

Deciding no Tarzan swing was complete without the famous ape man bellow, Rock gave his best "AHHHH AHH AHH AHHHH AH AH AHHHHHH" and cringed at the way his puberty-challenged vocal cords cracked and squeaked out the last bit.

His hands stung a little from the death grip he had on the rough rope and his eyes were once again tearing up—*I'm NOT crying! I just forgot to wear goggles again!*—but the swing was perfect. He knew then what Tarzan must feel like when he flew through the jungle from tree to tree like a monkey. Rock felt just like...a monkey. Safe in Mother Nature's bosom.

As he flew toward tree number two, eyes on the second rope he was to grab, Rock mentally applauded their efforts to get the ropes exactly the right distance from one another and to use ropes that had the right strength to hold his body weight.

But Rock was horrified to realize that, once again, the boys' planned stunt wasn't all that well thought out when he heard a sharp "CRACK!" and found himself hurtling to the ground with his hands still holding the rope, feet still firmly clinging to the knot in the end.

His life once again flashed before his eyes—which only took a few seconds since he was only thirteen—and Rock had time to contemplate the fact that the other end of the rope was still attached to the branch. Unfortunately, the branch was no longer attached to the tree. Mother Nature apparently didn't want him nuzzling around in her bosom.

In a way that would have made a great Roadrunner and Coyote cartoon (he decided then he really needed to quit watching so much television), Rock crashed through the trees, hitting a few branches on his way back to earth—which caused him to flip around but also helped slow him down—and hit the ground flat on his back with a loud "WHOOSH" as the air left his lungs.

As he lay there, making "eep eep" sounds whilst trying to get air back into his collapsed lungs so he could yell from the pain coming from his left arm that was bent at a funny angle, Rock stared in horror as the broken branch, which still had the roped tied to it, closed in on him. He wished then he had a little sign to hold up that said, "Oh Sh…"

Results: One broken tree branch; one broken left arm.

First Taste of Fast

At the ripe ol' age of fourteen, Rock decided backyard stunts just weren't cutting it for fueling his budding adrenaline addiction. He needed something more dangerous than just jumping inanimate objects; something more thrilling than trying to avoid getting caught by neighbors whilst inadvertently destroying private property and freaking out their pets; something more adventurous than reenacting Wile E. Coyote's crash and burns.

So he decided to start stock car racing.

Back in the day, that being the mid to late seventies, parents had no qualms about letting their barely teenage children climb into a tin can and race around a dirt track at breakneck speeds with no more safety equipment than a helmet and a seatbelt. Of course, this was the time that Smokey and the Bandit was the epitome for crazy driving and the shove it in "the man's" face attitude.

Now Rock's granddaddy was a former moonshiner, as in "I was there when NASCAR got started cuz the moonshiners had the fastest cars and could outrun any cop." Oh, you didn't know NASCAR was started by a bunch of drunk good ol' boy moonshiners? Well, ya learn something new every day, huh?

By this time, said granddaddy was somewhat of a respectable business owner—as respectable as a Jack-Daniels-drinking, chain-smoking, curse-words-for-punctuation, crusty ol' retired Air Force officer (well, technically it was the "U.S. Army Air Forces" back in WWII) could be —and was frankly too old to do much racing. Not that he'd ever admit that, of course. But other than speeding to make it to the liquor store before it closed, granddaddy didn't go fast much.

Granddaddy's only child was Rock's uptight mother, who certainly had never been interested in race cars or greasy mechanic types. Not her cup o' tea. Her cup o' tea leaned more toward fancy dinners at expensive restaurants and maybe a night of dancing at some joint fancy enough to be called a "ballroom." Needless to say, she definitely wasn't interested in racing, stock car or otherwise.

So the "go fast or go home" legacy apparently skips generations and was passed on to Rock, who was more than happy to take on the persona of reckless, crazed maniac behind a wheel. After all, what puberty-stricken male wouldn't jump at the chance to hop into a death trap and drive at insane speeds around a dirt circle with other similarly brainless hormone-challenged males? (Sorry, ladies, no offense meant here, but the gals just didn't race back then. They were too busy greasing up their legs to squeeze into those ultra skintight jeans so popular back then. And frankly, those legs just wouldn't bend enough to get into a race car. This was, after all, before stretch jeans were invented.)

Granddaddy bought a stock car for the sole purpose of having something for his grandson to drive. It was a'67 Plymouth Belvedere painted such a horrendous color of blue that the birds wouldn't even poop on it. It was so ugly that no one would park next to it for fear that it would somehow rub it's gruesomeness on their car. The car was just so hideous that cops wouldn't even pull the car over (which actually came in real handy). You get the idea —it was butt-ugly. Seriously.

After some minor repairs to the butt-ugly monstrosity—new tires, shocks, a carburetor rebuild, new engine mounts, a complete rewire with a new distributor cap—which then required getting a new battery, alternator and starter motor; so basically rebuilding the car from the ground up—the car was ready for tearing up the track.

Granddaddy was friends with the race track owner, who happened to be another hard-drinking, smoking and cursing old fart, and called in a favor to get some practice time in on the track before Rock's first race. The track owner wasn't that good of friends with Granddaddy, though, and so they only got an hour. Not much time for a kid who'd never driven a car in his life to learn what the slightly important things like a brake pedal were for, plus learn how to maneuver the death machine at break-neck speeds around slick dirt-packed corners.

Apparently Granddaddy wasn't too concerned about his only grandson's safety, since he figured the kid "would do just fine" after his whopping hour of practice and signed him up for a race coming up the next weekend.

The big day came and Rock was terrified. Not that he'd admit that, of course. No, no, he was a *man*, darn it, and had the facial hair to prove it—okay, so it was just one hair and it may or may not have been a cat hair that had gotten stuck to his chin when he had eaten that Laffy Taffy—and no fear was going to conquer his determination to get into the cockpit of that race car and propel himself at death-defying ("defying" hopefully being the operative word here) speeds around a racetrack that was starting to look more like the Cage of Death he'd seen at the circus last year.

Granddaddy walked up to the car while Rock was sitting in the lineup, waiting for the race to start. Rock straightened up in the seat. *Oh good, here we go. He's gonna give me that great advice he's been holdin' out on. Gonna tell me how to win the race. How to stay safe...*

The old man hocked a loogie on the car's back tire, then put his hand on the roof while he leaned down to impart his sage wisdom. He first graciously wiped the spittle from his mouth with the back of his hand.

"Don't crash and die, boy. Your grandma would kill me." And with that, the old fart walked off.

Rock sat in stunned silence. That was it? Seriously? What happened to all the wisdom of the ages that he'd been hoping for? Well, Grandaddy was as old as—well, as old as something really old—and he should know what he was doing, so Rock figured he'd better pay attention to what he had said.

Crash and die...crash and die. No! He said DON'T crash and die. He straightened again in his seat and squared his shoulders. *Okay, I can do that. I think. I mean, I am protected in this car, right?* He looked around at the cars in front of him and beside him. The other cars were made the same way...*So if two cars made of the same stuff crash into each other, what happens? On Dukes of Hazzard they crash cars all the time and just walk away, right? But that's TV. That's not real, is it?* Rock shrugged. *I don't know...but I do have this cool helmet and this stupid jumpsuit that makes me look like Captain Nelson on I Dream of Jeannie...and not when he was going into space. It's like that dumb thing he wore around the base. It's like a baby's jammies...*

Rock shook his thoughts aside. He had a race to race, darn it. He needed to focus. *Focus, focus, focus...Focus—what a dumb word. I mean, seriously, does it stand for something? Is it like short for something like Find Object Center Use Senses? No, that's dumb. That doesn't even make any sense. It's probably more like Flying Obstacles Coming Up Soon.*

He shook his head again. *Concentrate.* There, he'd just use a different word than "focus." But then he remembered a joke he'd read on a popsicle stick the day before: *"Why did the dumb kid stare at the can of frozen juice? Because it said concentrate."* Rock started laughing. That joke was still funny. The laughs turned to snorting giggles when he tried to stop and then he farted, which, as any male knows, automatically makes everything funnier.

When the snorting giggles turned to full-blown non-stop snorts, which then turned into hiccups, Rock realized he was starting to get a little hysterical. That wouldn't do. He needed to get it together; *act like a man, for Pete's sake.* He gripped the steering wheel a little tighter then and frowned, trying to burn a hole into the car in front of him. A few more giggles escaped, but he cleared his throat and stared harder.

Maybe if he really *concentrated*—another round of giggles followed that thought—he might be able to actually burn a hole into Bobby Ferguson's cherry red'77 Chevy Impala. Maybe even burn a hole right into his gas tank and then Bobby wouldn't be able to win the race, like he had every other race so far this year, thanks to his rich dad who bought him all the best stuff and probably had illegal modifications done to his car so that he could win. At least, that's what Grandaddy always said.

Rock's attention was caught then by a girl walking out onto the track with a green flag in her hand. She had long blonde hair and a really nice set of perky—*Hey! Is that Tom's sister? No, maybe not. Sure looks like her, though. Man, I remember that time me and the boys saw her take her bikini top off when we climbed that tree...*

Clearing his throat and wiggling to sit up straighter in his seat, Rock forced his thoughts away from those memories, or else he'd never be able to turn the steering wheel due to a, um, an obstruction. Well, in his barely-a-teenager mind, he thought that would be the case, but we all know better.

So back to the race. The girl with the perky—*don't go there*—held the flag high in the air and with a grin and a wink, threw it down. *Oh geez, here we go*...Rock may or may not have peed in his pants a little just then.

The cars all took off from the starting line like a herd of elephants trying to get to the only watering hole in the Sahara. Or like a herd of new mothers stampeding to a blue light special on diapers. Rock stomped on his gas pedal and shot forward with the rest of the pack.

Okay, so far so good. Of course, he'd only gone about thirty feet, but hey, at least he'd remembered which pedal was the gas. This time.

The first turn was coming up and Rock gripped the steering wheel even tighter. This was it, the moment of truth, the deciding factor on whether he was, or was not, in fact, a race car driver.

He thought back to his granddaddy's words...*"Don't crash and die."* No, no, no, not those words. The other ones...what he had said that morning over a bowl of Malt o' Meal: "When you get to the turns, stomp on it." *Stomp on what? The brake? Yeah, that makes sense. I would want to slow down for the turns, right?* But he noticed none of the other cars were slowing for the turn. In fact, it seemed like they might be actually speeding up, with their back ends coming out and the cars' noses pointing down toward the infield.

Stomp on the gas! And so he closed his eyes (briefly) and punched the pedal to the metal. The car surged forward and he turned the wheel to the right—thankfully he remembered that. It made no sense to turn the steering wheel in opposite direction you wanted to go, but hey, whatever. The old man knew better than he did.

He felt the back end slide up toward the stands while the nose pointed toward the infield. Just like the other cars. *I did it!* Rock may or may not have "yeeeehawwwwed" at this point. Probably did.

Okay, so since turn two came right after one, he remembered to keep the wheel hard right to just spin right on around and then thankfully also remembered to straighten his wheels back up when he came out of the turn. *Whew, that was fun...* He definitely "yeeeeehawwwwed" that time. But he still had turns three and four to navigate. And he had to do that over and over like a million times before the race was over.

Turn three came up pretty fast, but he made it around with no problem. If he could have taken a hand off the wheel, he would have patted himself on the back. Heck, he was starting to drive like an old pro now. In fact, he was absolutely pro material. Forget the Hollywood minions looking for new stuntmen—instead, he started fantasizing about NASCAR scouts in the stands, drooling while watching him drive and leaping over the bleachers so they could run to the pay phone (yeah, remember, this was back before cells) to call the team owners and tell them they found the next greatest Richard Petty. Fist fights would break out over who got to use the phone first and general mayhem would ensue.

Rock was so sure that he was going to be the next Petty that he even imagined having trophy girls fighting over who got to kiss him after he won his races. Yeah, they'd be clawing and scratching and crying over just who got to plant those red lipstick kisses on him. Rock imagined telling them, "Ladies, ladies, there's no need to fight. There's plenty of Rock to go around."

He was still fantasizing about NASCAR and trophy girls and kissing when he realized too late that he was coming into turn four. He frantically stomped on the gas and jerked the wheel to the right. But since he hadn't been paying attention and was already in the corner, his back end slid out and hit the wall, which caused him to spin around and hit another car. He thought he saw a flash of cherry red and had an ugly thought—*good, hope that was Bobby. Stupid, spoiled rich kid*—just before the car made another complete spin, hit the wall once again and then flipped.

As he was airborne, Rock once again saw his life flash before his eyes. Well, that and the sky, the ground, the sky, the ground again, the sky, the people in the grandstands—*Oh, I didn't know they sold Icees at the concession stand!*—then a bone-jarring, jaw-breaking slam into the ground as the car landed on its roof.

His first thought was that Granddaddy was going to kill him for messing up the car. And then he thought about how his mom was going to kill the both of them when she found out he'd been racing. If he had to go to the hospital, there was no way to deny it. She'd figure it out. Mom might be mean, but she wasn't dumb.

But then Rock realized that he was hanging upside down and he had a sudden vision of flames and burning, twisting metal—and burning, screaming Rock—so he frantically fought the release mechanism on the seat belt, crashed down to the roof and then scrambled out of the car's window.

Flipping through the air end over end several times is apparently the racing equivalent of that ride at the carnival with the cages that spins you up and around and over and over until you puke, because by the time Rock squeezed out of the slightly crushed window frame and stumbled out onto the track, he was dizzier than a cat who'd gone through a wash cycle in the Kenmore.

As Rock stood weaving and bobbing and looking like Granddaddy did after he'd tried to prove he could still out-drink everyone at the bar one night, he noticed something strange: He was seeing two of everything.

Rock had regained enough of his bearings at that point to realize that he was standing in the middle of the racetrack—and that said track still had moving vehicles traveling along it. He tried to get off the track then, but really wasn't sure which way to go since he'd been shook, rattled and rolled and he made the mistake of heading toward the grandstands.

Wow, there's a huge crowd here, he thought as he tried to make his way toward the lady he'd seen holding the Icee cup. He forgot that he was seeing double, but remembered that fact when he saw two granddaddies running down the side of the track and waving frantically at him, yelling something that sounded suspiciously like, "Get off the track, you idiot, or you're gonna get killed!"

It was then that Rock heard the motor and swung his head around to see that there were two cherry red Chevy Impalas coming right at him.

The yellow flag had been dropped, which meant "caution, slow down." Of course, for teenage boys the yellow flag sometimes also meant "pretend you didn't see it and try to get to the front of the pack." Which didn't work, because the officials "froze the field" whenever the yellow flag dropped, but most of the boys didn't know that fact.

Bobby Ferguson should have known that fact though, because he'd been racing for a full eight months by that time, so maybe he didn't see the flag. Or maybe he just didn't care about that caution flag, because he wanted to get back at the rotten son-of-a-so-and-so who dared to dent and scrape his shiny red car.

Regardless of how and why, Bobby Ferguson came around turn two way faster than he should have and didn't slow down, not even when the stumbling, bobbing Rock did a wide stance spin right in front of him.

Rock wasn't really hurt in the crash, thankfully. He'd just gotten spun around a bunch and had his marbles rattled. But his injury-free state changed the moment he made contact with the grill of that pretty Impala and did a fancy flip in the air that Tarzan would have been proud of, before landing on the roof of that shiny red car and rolling off the trunk, hitting the track with a dirt cloud that would have made Wile E. Coyote weep.

Results: One crushed hand, a handful of broken ribs, yet another concussion and a mouthful of dirt.

Antifreeze Brains

Sometimes being a daring stuntman in your own backyard just isn't enough fun and you get the urge to share your awesomeness with others. Spread your wings, so to speak.

Because authority figures rarely recognize the amazing talent it takes to be a true stuntman, phone calls get made and terms like "crossing state lines" get thrown around. If you're an underage stuntman, parents will be brought in and occasionally the police like to freak them out with words like "charged as an adult" and "third strike, you're out."

On one such occasion of being bored with their own playground, Rock and friends decided to head to Colorado to do some inner tubing. Apparently, Colorado has some sort of contract with Mother Nature that calls for magical snow to fall that makes skiing and tubing so much better there, or so the boys heard.

Being immortal wannabe teenagers and not prone to making the wisest and best choices, the guys fueled up their cars with gas and their bodies with Jack Daniels and headed out. Without bothering to tell any parental figures.

Several bottles of Jack later, the boys found themselves on the side of the road somewhere in the middle of the cold and snowy Rocky Mountains discussing just how freaking awesome it would be to tie all their inner tubes together to make a train.

Now, most sane people go to officially designated areas that have been safety inspected and approved in order to participate in such dangerous activities as propelling oneself down an icy slope on nothing more than a rubber donut with your butt bouncing just inches from the frozen ground and all the rocks and tree stumps that can be found there. Those designated places have safety precautions in place and areas mapped out for the safe enjoyment of such activities. It's the place where responsible people go in order to get a taste of the wild side, yet still feel confident that they won't die or lose a limb in the process. Or at least, won't bust their butt.

But Rock and the boys didn't want anyone telling *them* where they could tube, or how, or when. Heck, no. They also didn't want to have to pay the Forest Service fee, since they had spent most of their cash on booze and lunch at der Weinerschnitzel. Not to mention they didn't want any fellow tubers calling the cops because they were all in various stages of being falling-down-drunk.

So a private and convenient virgin slope on the side of the road is where they made their stop (actually, Kevin had to puke Jack and chili dogs, and when they pulled over to let him empty his gut on the pavement, the aforementioned virgin slope was just there, begging to be ridden like a…well, let's just say they all decided it was a destiny thing).

They were in a beautiful area with sparkling, pristine snow with a perfect, untouched top crust that would rival any professional baker's decorating, and came complete with a wide basin and a slope on the far end for hopefully preventing, or at least slowing, flying tubes. A few boys had to wipe a tear at the breathtaking beauty of the place. Well, it might have been fear causing the tear. 'Course, it could also have been from the aftereffects of puking one's chili dogs.

Back to the freaking awesome train thing. So someone said it would be cool, another agreed, yet another said "awesome" and KC, who at the time was heavily into Van Halen, said "It'll rock the house!" if they tied all six of their inner tubes together and then the twelve boys jumped on the train and rode that poor virgin slope, which they didn't realize in their whisky-foggy brains was seriously steep.

You can see it coming, can't you?

After much debate (which was in reality like three minutes), they decided the best virgin slope mounting technique would be to lay their train on the road, parallel to said slope. Then they could all drunkenly stumble to a tube, fall upon it, and rock and bounce the train to the edge and take off all at once.

Well, everything went according to plan, with the exception of Kevin The Lightweight having to puke yet again. The boys were all somewhat firmly planted on the tubes (some were suspiciously relaxed with their eyes closed and mouths open) when they started the rocking and bouncing process.

Several good bounces (and more upchucking, and not from just Kevin this time) later, the tube was at the very edge of the road at the top of the slope. The boys knew all they had to do was to lean slightly and the train would take off.

This is the point at which every stuntman (or brain-cell challenged inebriated teen) takes the time to reflect on the moment at hand, on the challenge before them, on death pounding rudely at their door. Thoughts fly through the brain like goose down feathers whipping out of a torn ski jacket.

"Geez, that's way higher than I thought." "Oh, crap...I really don't want to do this, but I don't want to wimp out." "ZzzzzzzzzzGRKKummphgrrkkkZzzzzzzz" (that was from one of those who had passed out). "This is going to be EPIC! I just hope Mom and Dad don't find out, especially since I'm still grounded for launching Mrs. Thompson's cat into the ditch. Seriously, isn't that why it's called a *catapult*?" (That was Rock, of course). "I think I'm gonna hurl." (Kevin the Lightweight).

So puking, snoring and wussing-out thoughts aside, someone counted down from five and the boys all tipped the train in unison. Well, sort of unison. It was more like one side went and the rest followed thanks to gravity and slippery snow. But regardless, down they went.

The takeoff was perfect, the train had a good tracking line and amazing speed (thanks to the grade of the slope that rivaled The Alps for steepness) and they had a perfectly clear shot to the bottom, across the basin and up the other side.

So what caused the train to derail and send boy bodies flying everywhere? Rock swore it had to be moving trees, like those giant ones in *The Lord of the Rings* book. Either God replanted the trees at the last minute, or they walked themselves over to the middle of the basin, but suddenly there they were, ruthlessly grabbing at tubes and boys, launching both in all directions.

The result looked like a scene from a B-rated horror movie, "Snow Trek, Wrath of Pine," "Nightmare on Pine Street," or maybe "Forest Dump." Regardless, the carnage was not something for weak stomachs. Of course, Kevin had to puke again when he saw it.

Results: Two torn inner tubes, several broken arms, contusions, concussions, and one severely fractured right leg (Rock's, of course). Not to mention the joy of having to call your parents and explain why you were drunk in a hospital in another state. While supposedly grounded.

Dirty Dancing

We now know that alcohol plus teenage boys plus hormone-charged brains minus common sense equals certain disaster.

Yet another case in point:

Rock had decided he was an adult at nineteen and moved to another state, much to the relief of his parents and the local police department. The only one who seemed to miss him was the county hospital, who sent him "Wish You Were Here" postcards every month or so.

He settled in an area known for its high-country rough terrain and populated by hard-drinking, loud-mouthed cowboys with testicles larger than their brains. Rock fit right in.

Everyone in the small town either worked on a farm or worked for a company that provided some service to farms and farmers. Rock chose the former, as a mechanic at a local shop.

Rock and his new set of brain-donor friends (they always manage to find one another and collect in groups, don't they?) decided to go to a local barn dance. Well, they really decided to drink copious amounts of alcoholic beverages while sitting in the back of Rock's truck and during the course of conversations consisting of "What do you want to do?" and "I don't know," someone mentioned the dance and that, unfortunately, became the plan for the evening.

Once they pulled into the makeshift parking lot (at a high rate of speed on two wheels, with boys standing in the truck bed, clinging to the roll bar with one hand and holding a Budweiser in the other), it didn't take long for the company of fools to realize that dancing while drunk and in the presence of the deodorant-detesting county lawman, Sheriff Rodgers (who never missed a dance or the chance to get alarmingly close to any unfortunate single lady) was probably not in their best interest, staying-out-of-jail-wise.

While they contemplated the other limited entertainment choices in the small town, which meant continuing the "What do you want to do?" conversations, Al had to take a leak. He stumbled over to a row of outhouses that had been conveniently positioned just outside of the barn along the top of a hill, then, after apparently deciding the door was too complicated to operate in his bobbing and weaving state, relieved himself on the ground at the base of the blue tower.

The boys hooted and hollered at Al, cheering him on when he shot a seemingly unending stream at the side of the outhouse, soaking it with yellow Bud-scented liquid.

"Hey, dummy, you're gonna flood the ground and send the stupid thing sliding down the hill!" Rock yelled, while the others hooted at that mental image.

Rather dim bulbs collectively went off over they boys' heads then, probably no more than twenty-five watt appliance bulb.

Surprisingly, the plastic outhouse structures are very slippery when tipped on their sides. They make for great modes of transportation.

And so, that is how outhouse surfing was invented. Well, the guys didn't call it an outhouse, but since I'm trying to keep this PG, I won't mention what they *do* call it (but the word starts with an "sh" and rhymes with "quitter." *cough*).

A steady stream of surfers flew down the hill, each trying to outdo the other for bravery (aka "stupidity"). There was the bull-riding routine, with Rock slapping the outhouse's sides with his legs like a Ty Murray clone, clinging to the handle and shouting "YEEHAWWWW!" Once, all the guys piled onto one outhouse and shot down the hill à la the Jamaican bobsled team. A few of the less drunk attempted to stand while flying down the hill, which more times than not resulted in a painful tumble through brush and cacti.

With a winch on Rock's truck, pulling the things back up the hill for the next rider was no problem at all. He had just finished getting one up the hill and was unhooking the chain from it when Maryann Peterson, second cousin of aforementioned stinky county sheriff, decided she needed to relieve herself of all the watered down punch she'd had and found herself without a place to do so. Rock tried talking her into using one of the outhouses while it was on its side, but Maryann wasn't game to try. Party pooper.

It didn't take long for the little snitch to alert the entire dance to the boys' antics, and soon the parking lot was filled with angry dancers, many of whom had suddenly decided they needed to use the facilities too. Al tried to engage the dancers in a "dance off" like in *Westside Story*, but didn't have any takers, despite his crouching and finger snapping efforts.

Sheriff Rodgers came out of the dancehall then and started yelling that the boys were all going to jail. But Rock hurried to unhook the winch chain from the outhouse and in an alcohol-induced-lacking-better-judgment moment, yelled "GET IN!"

Now, these boys grew up on Dukes of Hazzard—the original TV show, not the lame movie (seriously, Daisy Duke was *not* a blonde!)—and running from a sheriff seemed like a pretty easy thing to do. Maybe not the wisest thing, but simple nonetheless.

So yelling, "Hey, Sheriff, smell you later!" Rock threw the truck in gear and left the way they came—on two wheels with drunk boys clinging to the roll bar and cheering him on.

Rock hadn't lived in the area long enough to know all the back roads, and those who did know the area best were unfortunately in the back of the truck. Rock could hear Ricky yelling something about "curve" but couldn't quite make it out as he maneuvered the two-lane dirt road in excess of the sound barrier in his old half-ton Dodge.

It turns out the "curve" that Ricky was referring to was an S-curve at the top of a rather steep mountain. Not knowing this until the last minute, Rock had to make a dollar sign out of the S, heading straight through the trees and right into Mr. Malloy's barn.

Fortunately, they were going fast enough that the truck propelled itself right through the barn—to the astonishment of one cow and a handful of horses—and on out the other side, doing a few donuts in the field beyond before Rock got control of the truck. Well, as much as an inebriated, adrenaline-fueled teenager can *have* control anyway.

Amazingly, all the boys in the back survived the trip through the woods and barn and were still cheering Rock on, although some were cursing while pulling tree branches and barn mementos from their clothes. Rock stopped the truck behind the barn and turned the lights off, waiting to see if the sheriff was following.

The boys shouted in victory when the sheriff—who *was* well-acquainted with the back roads of his county—had slowed to make the curve the proper way and not via the new route Rock had just carved out and drove right by them.

Rock turned around and headed back the way they'd come, laughing at the stupidity of the sheriff. But something the boys didn't realize was that most counties employ a sheriff and at least one deputy. Most county vehicles have radios in their cars. Most deputies are more than willing to assist the sheriff at any time of the day or night. And most deputies also know the back roads of their county well. So, what the sheriff lost, the deputy found.

Results: Amazingly, no injuries, except to pride and pocketbook. Arrest record, judge-ordered fine of two hundred dollars apiece and community service in the repair of one barn and the replanting of trees. Plus Rock had to deliver a gallon of milk every other day until Mr. Malloy's traumatized cow decided to start lactating again.

Chapter 2 ALL GROWED UP, BUT AIN'T NO SMARTER

Here, Dear Deer

Surprisingly, Rock managed to survive his teen years, mostly thanks to an inordinate amount of luck and the talented staff at the local hospital.

His twenties didn't start off too good, however. But of course, this was due to less than well thought out decisions and friends who were even more common sense challenged than he. I know, it seems impossible, doesn't it?

One episode of "failure to use the lump two feet above one's butt," aka *the brain*, resulted in an injury to Rock that actually decommissioned him for quite awhile.

As I mentioned before, Rock came from the days when boys were boys, men were men, and hunting was the sincerest form of showing off the fact that you were filled with manly black-and-blue-colored testosterone. The guys were proud of that too and made fun of other guys who weren't so full of…testosterone. They figured it took a, uh, a *manure* load of girly hormones in a man to make him want to get a mani-pedi and carry a purse. Oh, excuse me…*a man bag*.

I digress. Back to our story. This particular injury-inducing, male-hormone-fueled adventure started out well, as they always do. These types of things like to do that to us—everything goes just right in the beginning, the way they were planned to do, lulling us into a sense of "everything's right with the world" serenity that will, of course, backfire like a'63 Studebaker with bad plug wires and sticky valves (or worse, like Billy Joe McPherson after the Jefferson County baked bean eating contest) and usually ends with a non-social visit with the local hospital staff, wearing a butt-exposing cotton gown and having a needle stuck in one's arm and a cast on some appendage.

Horace—or "Hoss" as the boys aptly nicknamed the overly large, not so bright, yet brimming with testosterone young man—and Rock decided to go deer hunting. Bambis were plentiful that year, having had a warm winter and wet spring that caused plenty of sweet wild grass to grow for the cute little darlings to munch on all summer and grow nice and plump. The boys couldn't wait to blast one or two between the eyes.

Now we've established that these guys were manly men complete with hairy chests and thickened foreheads from smashing beer cans, but you must also know that the black-and-blue-colored testosterone also has a tendency to cause laziness and has been responsible for such inventions as the motorized lawn mower and the battery-powered nose hair trimmer.

Such laziness was the cause of our hero's next injury. Well, laziness and the fact that Hoss was deaf in his left ear thanks to an unfortunate popcorn-in-a-pressure-cooker incident, but that is a subject for Hoss's book. This is Rock's book, so we'll stick with his side of things.

Rock at this time had a '77 Dodge Ramcharger. You remember those—you never saw them without the minimum of a six-inch lift kit, tires that would fit a semi, a winch bumper with a grill guard, KC lights and an air horn that would blow birds right out of the air (insert Tim The Toolman Taylor's awwr awwr awwr sound here)—they were the ultimate hunting beast.

So Rock and Hoss headed to the mountain and the designated animal murdering site with hopes of filling their freezers with enough meat to last the winter. Or, in Hoss's case, until Thanksgiving.

Picking a large meadow as the perfect site for the mass destruction of four-legged grass chompers, the boys parked behind a bushy area to wait them out. It didn't take long, with an entire herd soon making its way to the meadow and setting up a field perimeter for Operation Munch a Bunch.

As I said, deer were overly plentiful that year, so abundant that the insolent creatures didn't even bat one incredibly long lash of their big brown doe eyes when Hoss noisily relieved himself of a gas buildup caused by the toxic combination of teriyaki beef jerky and Mountain Dew. No, they just continued their systematic destruction of the grass, probably figuring there was safety in numbers. Deer aren't bright creatures. They probably have a lot of testosterone.

This is where the laziness factor came in. Since the deer weren't running from them, Rock got the twenty-five watt bulb idea to climb up on the hood of the Ramcharger and plant his feet against the grill guard, then point his cocked rifle at the bambis and have Hoss chase them down. That way, when the first shot rang out and the deer scattered, the boys wouldn't have to actually do any walking and or running to get deer number two.

Great plan, eh? Yeah, no.

Even though the herd has spent all spring and summer fattening up until they look a bit like toasted marshmallows with toothpick legs, they were surprisingly fast, once they realized there were two redneck mass murderers after them.

Springing through the meadow, the entire herd shot off towards the trees when Hoss barreled out of the brush with Rock yelling "Yeeeeeehawwwwww!" I don't know, don't ask me. I just write this stuff.

So the Ramcharger is bouncing over the meadow with Rock trying to hang on while still holding his rifle, Hoss is whooping and has the car stereo cranked all the way up playing AC/DC's "Highway to Hell" while the deer are bolting toward yonder tree line. The boys are quickly losing the race.

One overly chunky deer—who apparently had his own secret stash of extra fattening Twinkie grass—was waddling behind the rest of the herd, doing his best to get to the tree line before the maniacs caught up with him. Rock spied him and leveled his rifle, getting a rather rotund booty in his site, but he couldn't quite get a kill shot with all the bouncing going on with Hoss's erratic driving.

"Hurry!" Rock shouted over his shoulder, but Hoss couldn't hear him, what with Bon Scott's voice blaring from the radio.

"Hoss!" Rock turned to look at him and tried again. "Go!"

Now Hoss, being that he was deaf in the left ear, hung his head out the window and shouted, "What?"

"I said GO!"

Okay, admittedly, "go" does sound a little like "whoa," especially if one is trying to hear over the roar of a one hundred and five horsepower small block motor with Mr. Scott screeching "I'm going down, all the way down," (which, unfortunately for Rock, in the next few seconds would turn out to be a prophetic statement) and most especially if one is deaf in his left ear. So Hoss, sure that he heard "whoa" and being the obedient and eager-to-please friend, stomped on the brakes as hard as he could.

Remember how Rock was sitting on the hood with his feet planted against the grill guard? Well, once Hoss hit the brakes, Rock was catapulted and proceeded to somersault through the air like a Russian gymnast going for a gold medal.

And remember how Rock's rifle was cocked and ready to blow a poor, unsuspecting, helpless herbivore off his hooves? Well, after his fantastic feat of flying, flipping, free-falling and the inevitable flattening in the field, our friend's firearm fired. In the direction of the Ramcharger.

Thankfully for Hoss, who was in the direct line of fire for the small, but deadly, missile, a one hundred and five horsepower small block Mopar engine is just the thing to stop speeding bullets. Unfortunately, though, small block Mopar engines are not bullet proof, as the steam shooting from the radiator attested to.

The hiss the engine was making as radiator vapors escaped from the thirty aught six sized hole sounded like a death rattle to Rock as he lay in the meadow still clutching his rifle, making "eep eep" sounds as he tried to get air back into his lungs. His eyes, bulging from both shock and oxygen deprivation, moved from the billowing green cloud of steam to Hoss, who was now leaning out the window, his own eyes a bit bug-eyed.

"Dude…That. Was. Awesome!" His huge meat hook hand slammed the outside of the driver's door, causing Rock to wince, knowing he'd now have a dent to pull, on top of having to install a new radiator, get a new grill and Lord knew what else.

Hoss yanked the door open and leapt out, then stomped over to his buddy who was still eeping on the ground. Pushing his cowboy hat back, he leaned over and planted his bear paws on his knees.

"You okay, bud? You look a little green there."

Rock closed his eyes, knowing the green tint on his face was from the buildup of puke that was going to spew once he got enough breath back into his lungs to actually heave. Pain was wracking his body and he knew he wrenched his back, judging from the spasms running up and down his spine like a line of long-distance runners wearing golf cleats. Humans—well, other than those Chinese contortionists who probably have parts of their rib cages removed—are not meant to bend backwards the way he just did.

Results: Two hundred bucks for a replacement radiator and seventy-five for a new grill; six weeks laid up from a back injury; no venison in the freezer.

Building a Bad Rep

By his mid-twenties, Rock was married and a new homeowner. Well, a new used homeowner. A used home that needed a lot of work.

Being the manly man "I got this" sort and not one to ever even think about paying a professional to do the necessary repairs on his house, Rock would instead call on a friend to help when a job called for two sets of hands. Usually, said friend was equally manly and just as stubborn and sometimes a bit more clueless when it came to doing the things needing doing, but Rock's friends were always eager and willing to help their buddy out. Especially since it usually meant free beer and maybe even a free meal, if Rock's wife was feeling hostessish. No, that's not a word. Work with me, people.

Jerry was the lucky dude called upon to help out on the project that is the subject of our next fiasco. A little guy from the Ozarks, Jerry was a bit, well, shall we say, hillbillyish (yeah, I know, it's also not a word). He was never found without a wad of "chaw" in his cheek, was missing a front tooth (he claimed from a fight where he got sucker punched with brass knuckles, although his wife said he ran into an I-beam at work after consuming a six-pack for lunch), was never without a ratty John Deere ball cap shoved down over his always slightly greasy hair, and usually smelled of beer and pine tar, no matter the time of day or year.

So Rock called his greasy, smelly, tobacco-stained friend over to help him redo the old weathered porch of his house. Never one to leave a friend hanging, Jerry was all on that…well, the promise of a case of Bud didn't hurt.

It just so happened that Rock's grandparents were visiting at this time. Now, Rock's grandmother was a saint…you know, the type of woman that put up with a rotten husband for a bazillion years without complaint and always with a smile on her face. (She probably kept that smile because she knew all the dirty tricks she played on said husband when he was passed out. He just *assumed* all those bruises were from stumbling around drunk the night before. Little did he know his wife had a cricket bat hidden in her panty drawer…but I digress.)

Granddaddy, if you remember, was a crusty old fart, a hard-drinking, cuss-to-make-a-sailor-blush, don't take crap off nobody, old school of hard knocks kind of guy. A man's man. The kind who knows everything and isn't afraid to tell you that you're a moron for doing it the wrong way…*wrong* being any way you do it other than the way he told you to.

"That roof ain't gonna hold someone your size, boy," Granddaddy crawled as he eyeballed the porch.

"Best stand on the ladder to do the work."

Rock turned his head then at the sound of a truck pulling up, thankful for the interruption of the lecture. As usual, Jerry was arriving bright and early at the crack of noon. But as he hopped down from his overly lifted Ford, he seemed ready to take on the project, although Rock thought he looked a little unsteady on his feet, probably thanks to partying the night before...and the hair of the dog he'd probably consumed before heading to Rock's.

Rock growled at him for being late, but Jerry ignored his friend as he grabbed all the necessary roof-fixing tools—hammers, nails, Skil saw, beer cooler—and hauled them up the ladder. Rock was forced to stay on the porch because he was getting more valuable, yet annoying, instructions from his time-weathered and already slightly drunk Granddaddy. Rock thought Jerry was in good company.

After being told exactly how he needed to fix his own roof, where, and in what order, Rock climbed up the ladder to get started.

Stepping carefully onto the sagging roof, Rock was glad to see Jerry had managed to get everything up the ladder by himself, including the lumber. He rolled his eyes when he noticed Jerry was sitting on the cooler drinking a beer, an empty can already by his feet.

As mentioned, Jerry was a little guy, not weighing more than Rock's tool belt and that was only if he were holding a six-pack in his hand. Rock, on the other hand, is a big guy, and what was in his pants weighed more than Jerry and his six-pack. His keys and spare change, people. Keepin' it PG here. Sheesh.

The sagging porch roof was weathered and old, with cracked beams and rotting timber. Hence, the need for repair. Unfortunately, the roof was also unstable and unsteady and while it held Jerry, the extra lumber, tools and beer cooler, when Rock added his own weight, it made a loud CRACK. Rock just had time to snap his head up at Jerry in alarm before plunging through the newly created Rock-shaped hole he'd just made.

Fortunately, Rock wasn't hurt when he fell through the and managed to land on the porch below without injury, other than to his pride. He had a nanosecond to lay there on the weathered redwood, staring up at the hole he'd just come through and wondering how he'd managed to take such a fall and end up unharmed, when a shadow appeared at the hole and Jerry's bug-eyed faced peeked through.

"Whoa, dude, are you okay?" Jerry managed to croak out in his rather squeaky girly-man voice before turning to hock a pint of tobacco juice at the deck…right next to Rock's head. He wiped his mouth with his sleeve before continuing.

"That was a pretty…"

CRACK! Even though Jerry weighed little more than a third-grader, the already cracked wood decided at that moment to continue its imminent destruction and created a larger hole, this time large enough for all the tools and lumber to fall through. On top of Rock.

Curling into a ball and managing to protect most of his vital parts from the death rain of construction supplies, Rock grunted as each item hit him. First the hammer, then the Skil saw, the level, several two by fours, another hammer. But then the box of nails tipped at the hole in the roof and instead of falling as one box, proceeded to rain down from twelve feet above like mini-harpoons, stabbing the poor beached Moby Rock while he flopped and floundered helplessly like a, well, a fish out of water.

Of all the things sliding toward the hole in the sagging roof, Jerry chose to save the cooler. Which was probably the only thing that stopped him from landing on top of Rock, because as he lost his footing and slid toward the hole, the cooler cocked sideways across the hole, leaving Jerry dangling like a piñata by the cooler's handle.

Rock, still moaning and flopping and plucking little harpoons from his skin, happened to look up to see what else was going to crash down on him. When he realized it was his pint-sized friend and, more alarmingly, a cooler full of ice and beer cans, he quickly rolled to the side and out of the way, just in time for the roof to give way and release its hostage…and the rest of its structure.

Now, it wasn't just the roof that was old, weathered, sagging and in need of repair. No, the deck also had seen better days. So while Jerry and Rock rolled around on the deck, trying to avoid falling timber, the wood below them was also cracking and splitting ominously, apparently not up to the challenge of all the extra weight suddenly crashing down on it.

Let's stop a moment and discuss the lay of the land. Rock's new-used house was built in the mountains, on hilly terrain. The house itself was sitting on a fairly flat section, but the back yard was the upslope of the mountain and the front yard was the down slope. Which meant the deck was fairly high off the ground, about twenty feet or so. Twenty feet to the *ground*. The steeply sloping ground. You get the picture. And a sense of what's coming.

So back to the old, weathered, sagging deck in need of repair. Rock and Jerry were just laying there on the rotting timber once all the bits of roof stopped coming down on their heads, and contemplated first, their injuries and shocking lack of; and second, the question of just how shook up the beer cans might be (this of course was Jerry's foremost concern).

"Dang, that was lucky," Rock wheezed, since he still hadn't managed to completely fill his lungs. It was truly a miracle they hadn't gotten maimed.

"Yeah," Jerry agreed. "I can't believe the cooler stayed closed.""

Rock turned to his friend with a look that said, "You're a bigger idiot than I thought," and he started to say the words he was thinking when the porch gave another creak and groan. The two buddies snapped their bug-eyes at each other, knowing what was coming next.

The porch decided at that moment to release its new occupants, that being Rock, Jerry, the beer cooler, all the assorted tools, lumber and the rest of the porch roof, and puked them out like the contents of Rocks stomach last week after he'd gotten a bad batch of carne asada at Ruben's on Taco Tuesday.

Surprisingly, the boys survived the twenty foot plunge to the ground. But, like so often happens in a tornado, it's not the storm that gets you, but the debris. As they hit the ground, Rock on the bottom and Jerry sprawled on top of him, the assortment of crap that had fallen through the roof with them came tumbling down.

Just like a bad sit-com, the inevitable happened: The sixteen ounce hammer came flying down and whacked Jerry in his wife's favorite toy, that being the family jewels. When that little bit of bad karma happened, Jerry sat straight up, whacked his head on a support beam and knocked himself out. Which, of course, caused him to fall back and crack Rock in the face, breaking his nose.

Rock managed to roll Jerry off his chest and started at the stars and pretty little tweeting birds flying in front of his eyes for a few minutes when he noticed Granddaddy standing at the edge of the hole in the porch floor, cigarette in one hand, glass of Jack Daniels on the rocks in the other.

"Ya a'right, boy? Told you that roof wasn't gonna hold you."

Results: Rock and Jerry, concussions; Rock, broken nose; broken Skil saw; complete new roof and porch needed to the tune of two thousand dollars; Jerry's lack of ability to have sex and/or father children (for at least a week anyway); three-quarters of a case of Bud, shaken.

Chapter 3 IT'S THE LITTLE THINGS THAT'LL KILL YOU

Baby Blues

At one point in his life, Rock decided it would be the adult and responsible thing to get married and have children. It is those types of decisions by people like Rock that have caused more civilized and sane people to throw terms like "forced sterilization" around.

Regardless of the nay-sayers, Rock was the proud daddy of a brand-new, squalling, keep you up'til all hours, bouncing baby boy.

Now, for some insane and yet to be determined reason, the mother of said brand-new child decided she wanted some "me time" and thought it would somehow be a good idea to leave the common sense challenged baby daddy in charge for a few hours while she got away. Of course, this is Rock we're talking about—the man who was known for making less than brilliant decisions when it came to operating anything more complicated than a garden hoe. I do believe said mother was, in fact, common sense challenged herself.

I have to give the woman some credit, however; she did make sure that her grandmother, who lived next door, was home and was willing and able to be at the ready should an emergency occur, such as the selfish desire of the baby to be changed and fed.

Rock had told his wife that watching his son was no problem at all, just how hard can it be? You change a diaper, feed him a bottle, he goes to sleep, easy peasy. I'm sure she was just a bit hesitant as she walked out the door, knowing her husband's penchant for trouble. But the silly woman decided to leave anyway.

About two point three seconds after Mom's car pealed out of the driveway like a stunt driver from *Fast and Furious*, the baby decided to start screaming. And Rock started twitching. The mother of his screaming child had a head of fiery red hair with a matching temper and if she came back from her mini-vaycay to find a blustering baby, Rock knew he'd be dodging frying pans and maybe even knives. She was one scary female.

Now the first plan of attack when dealing with a fussy infant is the lower half, so Rock assumed the baby needed changing. Juggling baby, a diaper and a box of wipes, Rock carried him to the bedroom where the changing table was and tried to reason with the child.

"Shhh, we'll get you changed in just a sec. No need to yell, okay? Seriously. Why are you screaming? I've peed my pants lots of times and never cried about it. Wait, don't tell your mom about that, okay, bud? That'll just be our little secret. Dude, seriously, you should stop crying now. I'm changing you. You'll be dry in just...oh, crap! Don't pee when I take the diaper off! Now look what you did. You got piss all over me, the table and your face. No, no, no! Don't cry more! It's okay, we'll just use the wipes to clean your face. Well, *now* what the heck are you screaming about?"

Unfortunately, brand-new infants are stubborn creatures and don't respond well to rational reasoning or parental frustration, and the baby started screaming even louder. Which, of course, made the dog start barking. And apparently a dog's bark is some sort of a turbo switch for a screaming infant, which enables them to increase the decibel level of their anger to a pitch capable of shattering the windows in low-flying aircraft passing overhead.

Rock, in usual new daddy fashion, panicked, certain the baby was going to break blood vessels—if not his own, than surely the ones in his father's ears. And probably the dog's, too, who by this time was howling in pain and slamming into walls, most likely in an attempt to rid his head of what was surely a group of hellish demons that had started an acid metal rock band and were practicing in the two-car garage between his ears.

Starting to wonder if the baby was really an alien and the screaming was his way of reaching outer space in order to call the mother ship to come rescue him from his miserable existence on the third rock from the sun, Rock struggled to come up with another idea to stop the imminent destruction of his planet.

Plan B in dealing with a fussy—or insanely out of control—alien infant is make the top half happy. The appliance bulb went off over his head just then. "Bottle!"

Rock flew down the hall and ran into the kitchen, sliding past the refrigerator on the slick linoleum and crashing into the china hutch next to the sink, which teetered precariously, his wife's heirloom china tipping against rails and the crystal trinkets that lined the top rocking dangerously. Rock threw his arms and body up to hold the thing steady.

Junior chose that moment to increase his screams yet another few decibels, which Rock was sure was designed to create a new hole in the ozone layer for more direct Earth-to-space communication. At the very least, it was going to cause the San Andreas fault line to finish cracking, releasing the continent's hold on California, allowing it to become the latest addition to the Hawaiian islands.

Leaving the still rocking hutch, Rock slid back to the fridge, yanked the door open and grabbed one of the premade bottles mom had left behind. Baby was now screaming and hiccupping, which made Rock worry that he was causing permanent damage to his lungs.

He was also rethinking his decision to leave the baby alone on the changing table with the howling dog still in the room slamming into every object in his blind-with-ear-pain path, and the sudden picture of the dog crashing into the changing table entered his mind. So he jerked the door open on the ancient microwave that his grandparents had given them and tossed the bottle in.

Now, his granddaddy had bought the microwave in the early seventies from a government surplus auction. It was probably used in science experiments, testing the effects of radiation on such things as aluminum cans and earthworms. But Granddaddy had bought a new and improved, never before used in a laboratory microwave, and donated the old one to his grandson and wife. It was ancient, but it worked...and if you ignored the way your skin tingled if you stood too close when it was running, it was a fine appliance. Rock spun the dial on the contraption, hit the start button, and ran back down the hall.

Thankfully, the baby was fine—if "fine" is defined as lying flat on ones' back and calling to one's people stationed at a galaxy far, far away at decibels never before heard. Rock snatched him up, trying to shush him while also trying to keep his own eyeballs from melting as the screams were now just inches from his eardrums.

"Shhh little dude, it's okay. You don't need to call the mother ship. You'll like Earth, promise. Once you get past this boring baby stage, we'll get to do all kinds of cool things, okay? Like building race cars, racing, crashing… okay, don't tell Mommy about the crashing part. She'd probably bash my head with that big cast iron skillet she uses for chicken fried steak. No, no, it's okay. Your bottle is in the microwave, warming up just the way you like it. We'll get you earthly sustenance in a sec, okay?"

If you've ever put a container with a liquid substance in the microwave while leaving the lid intact and then blindly spun the dial to say, oh, five minutes or so, then you know that the radioactive microwaves cause the molecules in the liquid substance to accelerate to light speed, and being in a closed container, said molecules have no way to vent (or something like that) and eventually something's going to give. (Okay, I pretty much made all that sciencey sounding stuff up, but it sounded good, didn't it?)

As I said, the microwave was old and probably leaked enough radiation to rival the levels at Chernobyl on a sunny day. And the flimsy door was designed with a small hook latch, not really very safe...nor effective in containing an exploding bottle of infant formula.

At this moment, Rock and the squalling alien had entered the kitchen, just in time to hear the explosion as the microwave door blew open, and witnessed what looked like a mangled Playtex bottle fly past them and hit the still unsteady china hutch.

The hutch containing his wife's precious and irreplaceable heirlooms was now beyond teetering and had moved to the next step of tipping, which caused the decorative crystal trinkets on top to take a death plunge to the floor below. One trinket must have decided to make a last ditch effort to save itself and changed its trajectory, crashing to the kitchen sink, where dishes from the spaghetti they'd had for lunch were still soaking. Some utensil apparently took exception to being slammed into by a hundred-year-old crystal turtle, and it flew up, hitting—and shattering—the kitchen window.

Rock, not knowing what to do since he was still holding the alien against his now completely and thankfully deaf ear, stood in abject horror, watching as the rest of his crazed, skillet-wielding wife's precious collection of family history headed toward destruction.

Now, in the typical too little too late fashion, next door neighbor Gramma Lizzie chose that very moment to investigate all the screaming and noise and opened the back door, just in time to see her own china plates—the set that her dear departed husband had brought back from France during WWII—hit the faded yellow linoleum floor and explode into a thousand brokenhearted pieces.

The alien, still hungry and sure that his salvation was only too be found within the mother ship, decided to increase his screams to yet another new level, which sent the howling dog out into the night through the open back door, never to be seen again, and making Rock realize that he just *thought* he had gone deaf in that ear, but had obviously been mistaken, as he was now sure blood was oozing from what had once been his eardrum.

Gramma Lizzie tore her eyes from the carnage, her eyes wide and her weathered face pale as she stared at her grandson-in-law and her great-grand-screaming-alien-creature. Rock wondered at the horrified look in the old woman's eye, thinking that this was the woman whose favorite sayings were "it's just stuff" and "you can't take it with you" and surely she couldn't be *that* upset about losing all her precious family heirlooms. Junior chose that moment to stop his squalling for a split second (presumably to get more air in his lungs for a brand new record-breaking assault) and that was when Rock realized what apparently had caused the look on the old woman's face…it was the sound of a car screeching into the driveway.

Skillet-wielding Mom, obviously having heard her screaming infant just before hitting the county line twenty miles away, had returned. Rock felt a bit faint, knowing his end was near. Death by cookware was not how he had pictured the end of his life. He had hoped for something a bit more manly.

Results: Over one hundred years of memorabilia destroyed; a suspiciously quiet alien baby once being held by its mother—prompting Rock to wonder if Mom was really an alien too; a concussion and "Wearever" imprinted on Rock's skull.

Repeat After Me: Power Tools Are Not Toys
Most fathers at one time or another have had moments of less-than-intelligent decision making times and have allowed their children to play with something dangerous—like giving said toddler a screwdriver, or maybe the kindergartener a circular saw.

Rock was no exception. He thought nothing of allowing his now school-aged child to tag along with him while doing chores around their ranch on his days off from running the local tire store. Such chores included simple things like feeding the livestock, fixing fence, clearing water lines, and reroofing a thirty-five hundred square foot house.

The day of the reroof started like any other—the sun came up (okay, technically, we all know that the sun doesn't actually *come up* and it is in fact the earth's rotation that causes this phenomenon, but I digress), people awoke and adults grumbled their way to the coffeepot while the kids bounced around from having a nighttime's worth of energy stored, needing release. The rooster crowed, the sheep baa'd and the cows moo'd—all sounds that meant "Get up, lazy humans, and feed us!"

Rock's father-in-law, Bart, had graciously offered his services to help install the roof on the house and had shown up bright and early, eager to get started on the project. Of course, the alien child—whom we'll call "Gravel" for the sake of continuity—was also eager to help, because, well, power tools.

After a hearty breakfast of Folgers and fat pills (aka "donuts") and then a ten minute argument with Gravel's little sister, Pebbles (you're getting the choice of names, right?) about the fact that four-year-old girls can't climb ladders and use nail guns, Rock and crew headed outside and gathered the weapons of mass destruction they would need to complete their job.

Rock had spent the previous afternoon loading all the sheets of plywood onto the two-story roof with the backhoe, so thankfully, that heavy job wouldn't need to be done. But they still had to haul up the circular saw, the nail gun, the giant box of nails and the cooler loaded with Diet RC and CapriSun. All while making sure the seven-year-old alien child didn't fall off the ladder. Or knock one of them off.

Bart led the way up the ladder while the always safety-conscious Rock (okay, so that's a total lie, but hey, even a broken clock is right twice a day) held the bottom of the ladder, then watched as young Gravel made his way up.

For some reason, during a less-than-bright moment, Rock had agreed to let Gravel carry the heavy box of nails up the ladder. Imagine a large-for-his-age-but-still-just-a-kid kid trying to maneuver up a ladder whilst hanging on to a fifteen pound box. Imagine this kid's parental figure standing fourteen feet below, yelling helpful encouragements such as, "Hurry up, daylight's burning" and "No, don't pick your nose. Boogers will make your hands slippery." Imagine the kid looking back down at said parental figure to argue that boogers, are in fact, not slippery but sticky, and then said kid losing his grip on the fifteen pound box of sharp pokey objects.

After Rock came back outside from getting a bandage for his bleeding forehead, he climbed up to the roof where Bart and Gravel were arguing over who should go back down the ladder to get the portable air compressor no one thought to take up with them.

Once Rock got back on the roof after retrieving the compressor, he plugged the air hose in and got to work nailing plywood to the roof while Bart used the circular saw to cut the wood to size. Gravel, of course, wanted to be helpful in some way, so Rock decided now was as good a time as any to teach his progeny to use a nail gun.

Seven-year-olds and any kind of weapon are usually a bad combination. But when a weapon shoots something sharp with bird killing velocity, well, heck, that's like having a knife *and* a gun all in one. Little boy holy grail.

Rock managed to save two birds who had been nailed to the big pine tree near the house—thankfully, Gravel's aim wasn't too great and only feathers were ruffled, since they were crows and not something anyone wanted to eat (who wants to eat crow?)—and once he returned to the roof where he'd so far only managed to get two sheets nailed down, he gave Gravel a lecture about just what he was allowed to point the nail gun at, and that wasn't anywhere but the roof.

"Here," he said as he pointed to the plywood he was holding in place, "this is what you can shoot. Right here."

You've heard the expression "famous last words" right? Well, when you tell a seven-year-old alien child with ADHD to "shoot right here," that's what you're gonna get. Even if your hand happens to be "right here."

Rock's roof-shaking yell when that nail went into his hand through the webbing between the thumb and forefinger was enough to send Gravel running—running right to Grampa Bart who was still cutting sheets of plywood and couldn't hear the commotion going on behind him.

A big for his age seven-year-old running in terror from his father who is nailed to the roof has quite a bit of force behind his momentum, a fact Bart found out the hard way. Literally.

Gravel, looking behind him at his still yelling father who was nailed to the roof by his bleeding hand and who was trying desperately to grab the hammer that was lying just out of reach, ran full force into his grandfather, causing the old man to lose his footing and step back onto the stack of plywood.

When a stack of flat items is pushed on from the top, the law of physics says that the stack will slide off from the top down. (That may or may not be a physics law, but let's just pretend, 'kay? And I cannot be held responsible for any science tests the reader may fail based on any sorta kinda true information given here.)

Apparently, Bart knew this might-be-true law, as he started trying to run backwards on the stack, sending sheet after sheet of plywood flying off the roof. Until he got to the bottom sheet, that is; then he proceeded to wobble and bobble until both he and the sheet went sailing off the roof like he was riding a flying carpet. Or, more accurately, a falling brick.

Gravel wasn't sure who was yelling louder—his father, who was still neatly nailed to the roof, or his grandpa, who was writhing on the ground two stories below screaming something about his "cock six," whatever that was. Regardless, Gravel decided that was a good time to go back in the house, make a sandwich and watch cartoons.

Rock yelled at the alien child as he watched the kid head to the ladder, but his loin fruit wasn't listening. Nope, he just plain ignored his old man. So Rock gritted his teeth against the coming pain and then scooted a bit farther down the roof to try to hook the hammer with his foot. Which of course pulled the nail deeper into his hand and a string of curses not heard since the battle of the three hundred Spartans left his mouth.

After releasing a gallon of pain-induced sweat (and maybe a little pee too), he finally hooked the hammer with the lace of his boot and carefully pulled the tool up where he could reach it with his unattached hand. Well, this hand was attached to his body, just not to the roof. Just in case there was any confusion. I never know just who might be reading this stuff, ya know?

Anyhoo, once he finally had the hammer in hand, he carefully—and excruciatingly—pried his hand from the roof...using the claw part of the hammer. Yeah, I know. Gross, huh?

Climbing down a ladder while hugging your throbbing, bleeding hand to your body is harder than it looks. Well, maybe not. It's probably just as hard as it looks, honestly. Once he got down, Rock checked on Bart to make sure the old man was still breathing—like he didn't already know that from the yelling, cursing and unnecessary mention of a lawsuit coming from him— Rock went inside to seek some sort of medical attention.

Now the woman Rock was married to at the time wasn't usually inclined to give him any sympathy, or help, for that matter, whenever he hurt himself. Remember, this is the Wearever-wielding psycho we're talking about. We'll call her Skillet from this point on.

This lack of regard for her husband may or may not have been due to the man's uncanny ability to find trouble wherever it may be hiding. Seriously, Rock could get hurt in a round room with walls padded with ten feet of cotton balls, lamb's wool and baby goose down.

Regardless, Skillet took one look at the father of her children, noting his pale complexion and somewhat teary eyes as he clutched his hand to his chest and with a shocked look of concern said, "Don't bleed on the carpet," and left the room.

Fortunately and unfortunately, Rock's mother-in-law, Beglenda (hey, her parents couldn't decide between Belinda and Glenda. Don't judge), had come over to the house that morning with her husband. It was fortunate, because the woman was nothing like her uncaring daughter and so when she came into the kitchen, she took one look at her bleeding son-in-law and immediately ushered him to a chair and started fussing over him. It was unfortunate, however, that the woman prided herself on being a natural healer, when she, in fact, didn't know much about healing at all.

Rock had a moment of conscience as he thought he should tell Beglenda that her husband was writhing on the ground outside with possible paralyzing back injuries, but frankly, he was enjoying getting all the attention for the moment. Bart could just wait.

Beglenda fussed over Rock, getting paper towels to wipe the blood, sweat and tears, then fetched him a glass of lemonade before she ran off to get her "medical kit" which mostly consisted of essential oils and assorted dead animal parts.

Here is where the "unfortunate" part of having Beglenda doctor him took over. Not really knowing exactly what she should put on a gaping hole in one's son-in-law's hand, she decided the safest course was to just mix a bunch of different oils and pour them in. To the open wound. Yeah.

Did you know that individually cinnamon, peppermint and eucalyptus oils will burn like a mofo when you pour them into a flesh hole? And that when you combine the three, it's the equivalent heat ratio of a ghost chile soaked in jalapeño juice and scorpion venom? No? Rock didn't know that either, not until about point two-four seconds after Beglenda taught him that lesson.

When his mother-in-law dumped that mix on his hand, Rock just had time to blink and then the unholy excruciation took off like a match to dried prairie grass. Fire. Blazing hell fire. Brimstone and molten lava. A steel smelter. On the surface of the sun.

Rock jumped to his feet and ran screaming to the sink.

Have you ever seen those videos where some moe-ron (gotta say it just like that for full effect) puts a frozen turkey into hot oil? You know that fire that shoots up thanks to the water on the turkey hitting the boiling oil and burns said moe-ron's house down? It's the premise behind Greek Fire. Pretty much the same thing happens when you put water on essential oils that are in the process of burning flesh to a charred crisp.

After taking his screaming to a whole new decibel level that had the Space Station calling NASA to complain, Beglenda managed to get Rock to sit back down so she could pour some more oil onto his hand—this time just plain ol' olive oil. Thankfully, that helped put the fire out.

"Now, let's see if you're gonna need stitches," she said as she tried to pry Rock's hand away from his chest.

"I don't need no (blankety-blank) stitches cuz you cauterized the dang thing with your blasted oils," he replied through gritted teeth. He didn't want to hurt the woman's feelings, but he was also sort of partial to his body parts and didn't want to take the chance she might want to use rabid cat's whiskers or the webbing from a venomous South American red-eyed jumping spider to stitch his wound. At this point, he just wanted her to leave him alone.

A sudden light popped up above his head then. Just like in the cartoons.

"Uh, Bart is outside. I think he's hurt too. Might want to check on him."

Now Rock would have smiled at the way Beglenda's eyes widened before she grabbed her bag of death magic and took off out the door like a dog with its tail on fire (or a dog who'd been dipped into a deadly essential oil bath), but he was still in too much pain to find anything funny.

But he did laugh when he heard Bart yell, "Leave me alone, woman! I ain't no witchy science project! I wanna go to the hospital! Dang it, listen to me! Wait, what are you doin'? What are those oils? How is that gonna...YEEEEOOOWWWWW!"

Did you know that cinnamon, peppermint and eucalyptus oils burn like Hades' fireplace when they run down your back and into the crack of your...

Results: One charred hole in hand that couldn't be stitched; one broken tailbone with a subsequent blistered booty crack; one full week of roofing time lost.

The View From Up Here

When you live on the side of a mountain in a pine forest, there comes a time when you must chop down a tree. Sometimes a tree gets eaten by beetles or the dreaded porcupines, or it gets a disease. Or sometimes it's just in the way of something you need to build or maybe you need firewood. Whatever the cause, cutting a tree down is a common thing for a mountain man and is a fairly routine process.

However, there is nothing routine about any process when you allow an ADHD-riddled, ten-year-old alien to help you. Rock just never learns. (Let's take a moment to shake our heads sadly here.)

The tree Rock needed to take down was a seriously tall pine that had attracted pine beetles and was on the verge of turning to sawdust all by itself. So before the tree crumbled onto some unsuspecting cow, Rock decided to take it down.

Now the safe way to bring down a tree that's grown to Eiffel Tower proportions is to take it down a section at a time. In a moment of sheer adult-like responsibility, Rock decided to do just that, and in an even further shockingly responsible moment, he actually thought to tie himself to the tree before sawing off the first chunk. I know, shocking, right? Apparently, he *was* capable of learning from his mistakes.

Oh wait...strike that last comment. We have forgotten about the alien child. The alien child who, in a moment of boredom that started about two point six seconds after his dad started climbing the tree, had discovered a two-man saw lying near the tree. Being a strapping young man who thought he was just as big and strong as his dad, he picked up the saw and decided to help his parental figure by working on the bottom while his dad worked on the top.

Rock of course heard the noise and looked down to see his son struggling to work the two-man saw. He smiled to himself, thinking how cute it was that the boy wanted to be like his old man. Rock wasn't concerned, because, seriously, how much damage was Gravel going to be able to do with something he could barely handle that weighed nearly as much as he did? Turns out, a lot.

It's amazing just what a bored, ADHD-riddled ten-year-old can accomplish when they set their little mind to something. Of course, said *something* is never homework or actual chores; no, that burst of determination is almost always reserved just for doing something they shouldn't.

Rock finally got to the top of the tree and tied himself off, then spent a few minutes trying to get the chainsaw started. By the time he finally got it started and cut through the tree top, Gravel had managed to cut about halfway through the trunk. With a handsaw. A *two-man* handsaw. Never, *ever* underestimate a bored alien.

Now when the top of the tree came off, the movement caused the rest of the tree to sway, which was exaggerated by Rock's added weight. And the swaying caused the freshly cut trunk to snap.

Let's go back to Rock's moment of unprecedented safety consciousness and remember that he had tied himself to the tree so that he wouldn't unexpectedly fall out of that tree. Having the trunk snap is an unexpected event that did cause him to fall out of the tree. Well, not technically. He was still attached to the tree, so he didn't fall *out* of the tree. But he did fall *with* the tree. All. The. Way. Down. Through about a dozen other trees. Trees with branches. Sharp branches. And pinecones. Really, really sharp pinecones.

Thankfully the tree he was attached to was a big tree, with big pine boughs. Also thankfully, the top portion that Rock had cut actually cushioned the fall of the rest of the tree. Sort of. Pine needles make a semi-soft landing pad. Sort of.

Pine needles also embed themselves in skin in surprisingly deep proportions.

Results: One tree downed much faster than planned; knowledge that aliens can saw a tree faster than a human; the realization that pine needles are, in fact, needley.

Shocking Revelations

Not long after the tree felling accident (okay, it wasn't an accident, but still…), winter came and with it, cold weather. Duh. So anyway, stock tanks tend to freeze in, uh, freezing weather and so smart ranchers will install heaters that prevent this from happening. Shockingly, Rock was one of those smart ranchers. I know, right?

One of those oh so helpful stock tank heaters decided to stop working. Nowadays, those things are mostly solar-powered, but back in Rock's day, they were electric. Rock, thanks to numerous other life lessons, knew just how shocking electricity can be and did the responsible thing by unplugging the heater before pulling it out of the tank to replace it.

It was a good thing he did unplug it, because once he removed the heater, he could see that the wires were cut through in one spot, probably due to a Hereford using it for a chew toy. And of course the heater was stuck in several inches of ice that had formed when the heater had gone out and Rock had to work pretty hard to get it out and of course got soaking wet in the process.

While his dad was rewiring the heater, Gravel, in typical "I'm bored waiting for Dad to finish" fashion, picked up some rocks and started throwing them onto the hard ice floating in the tank. After the third rock bounced and hit Rock square between the eyes, he growled at the alien child to "go find something else to do."

Wandering around the area and kicking at the snow, Gravel happened to notice a cord on the ground. He picked it up and started walking, following the cord to its starting point…which was the electrical outlet at the end of the fence.

Being the oh-so-helpful alien that Gravel was, he said to himself, "Self, this must be why Dad can't get the heater working…it's unplugged!"

Once Rock stopped twitching and could feel his fingers again, he managed to finish rewiring the heater, then got back on his horse and pulled Gravel up behind him.

"Try not to mess with anything else, okay son?" he asked while both eyelids twitched uncontrollably. He knew it was a request that would probably never be granted. The alien was just too active and got bored too easily. Rock added in the promise of taking the boy to town for burgers and fries if he'd behave until he could get his chores finished.

The cows had pushed a section of fence down and the boys headed over to see what they could do to fix it. Of course, this was the section that was electrified, but apparently cows like the shock of the fence in the cold weather—maybe it gives them enough of a tingle to warm their brisket—because they had pushed that section right on over.

Even though he was wearing thick leather gloves, Rock was very careful when he unplugged the bare wire that he'd rigged to electrify the fence with more current than he would have gotten from a normal—aka "safe"—set-up. He'd even wrapped the shock wire around the barb wire to help deter the cows from pushing the fence, but that didn't stop them. Apparently his cows also had trouble minding and needed a little extra discipline. He then gave a stern look to Gravel that told him not to mess with the wire and he went back to the cow-shaped hole and started pulling barb wire back up.

Rock was fighting with one of the more tangled pieces when he noticed Gravel had disappeared. Never a good thing with that boy, but at the moment Rock was too tangled up in sharp steel wire to worry about what the kid might be up to.

His fingers were still pretty tingly from the incident at the stock tank, so he pulled his gloves off to better feel the wire where the barbs were twisted together. It was well below zero that day and the muscles in his hands instantly cramped against the cold. Cursing, Rock put the barb wire wrapped with the shock wire between his teeth so that he could clench and unclench his hands to get the circulation going. Yeah, I know…who does that? Well,

Rock was a pretty tough guy, so barb wire in his mouth probably wasn't that big of a deal, except for the fact that his Copenhagen was getting caught in the barbs.

The wire wasn't cooperating, so he stepped on the bottom wire to hold it down so he could work on the next two strands up. When he had finally gotten those two separated, his boot slipped off the bottom wire and it sprung up and caught him just below the crotch, where it embedded in his jeans.

So there he was, top strand in his mouth, holding the next two strands apart so they didn't re-tangle, and unwilling straddling the bottom strand, when he heard the alien yelling something like, "Daddddddd, saaaaaave meeeeeee!" He turned as best he could to see what was going on, but since he'd become one with the fence, his turning radius left a lot to be desired. But there was no denying the panic he heard in his son's voice and knew nothing good was coming his way.

Sure enough, Gravel was running over the hill at the far end of the field as fast as his little legs could go, which wasn't very fast, considering the snow was as deep as his knees. Rock frowned, still not sure what the alien boy was running from, but then he noticed a cloud of steam coming from the back side of the hill. His frown turned to a puzzled scowl as he tried to figure out just what—*oh no…*

Soul Reaper, one of the ugliest, meanest and just plain evilest bulls ever to tour the Pro Bull Riders circuit, had been given to Rock when his owner retired him. Soul was worth a lot of money just for breeding purposes, but Bill, Soul's former owner and one of Rock's good friends, had had enough of the big dude's hatefulness and attacks and had given him to Rock in exchange for a set of new truck tires and a twelve-pack of Coors.

The bull was pretty old by that time and kind of beat up from years of rodeoing (no, that's not a word, but let's just go with it, okay?), but that didn't stop him from charging like a runaway freight train down a straight track when he was pissed. And at that moment, Soul was snorting steam and running straight for Gravel, who, Rock noticed just then, held a rather large stick in his hand.

Knowing the alien had probably thought it would be funny to whack the bull in the butt with the stick, Rock fought to get untangled from the wire so that he could save the boy—mostly from fear of what the mother might do to him if the kid got hurt, but there were some parental concerned feelings going on too. But mostly it was fear of mom. That fear made him struggle more furiously to get untangled…which of course just made everything worse.

Rock was nearly panicking by this time and hopped up and down, trying to jiggle the barb wire off his legs where it had wrapped like an amorous boa constrictor. The hopping only made the barbs release his jeans at the thigh so that they could bounce up right into his crotch and embed themselves in the family jewels. At that point Rock was yelping like a puppy with its tail caught under a rocking chair.

Gravel by that time had somehow managed to get his feet on top of the snow and was running like his life depended on it—which it probably did, since Soul Reaper was closing in on him fast. But the boy was closing in on the fence even faster where his father was working and leapt like an NBA forward going for a slam dunk.

He didn't quite clear the fence since his father was in the way, but he grabbed the top of the corner post and perched there like a vulture awaiting the imminent death of some dehydrated rabbit. The poor kid was gasping and his eyes were wide enough to startle a sloth.

But the fence post was snow-covered and slippery and Gravel's feet started slipping. He frantically grabbed at the post, the wire, his dad's head, but nothing saved him from taking a tumble off the post—fortunately, onto the bull-less side of the fence. Unfortunately, during his mad scrambling for balance—we think there may have been some unearthly mischief maker involvement here, like a leprechaun or Loki—Gravel somehow managed to reconnect the bare shock wire to the power source.

Now let's remember that Rock was holding the wires between his teeth and the rest of it was wrapped around his still-wet-from-the-stock-tank-incident body. Imagine what happens when you have an electrical current with the equivalent amperage of, oh say, airport runway lights, going through your mouth, your hands, your legs and your nether regions. All of which are wet.

Rock didn't stop shaking for about a week after that.

Results: Surprisingly curly hair and the ability to turn electrical appliances on from three inches away; one freezer full of former rodeo bull; an alien child who learned the hard way not to smack a three thousand pound bull on the booty; and thankfully, the inability to father further alien children.

Humpty Dumpty
The chimney was crumbling and Rock had to fix it "before Santa comes,

or he might get stuck and then he won't leave us no presents cuz we'll be on the naughty list and it'll be *all your fault, Dad!*" Or so Gravel and Pebbles informed their father.

Rock had the bright idea (think light bulb above the head again) to load the new bricks he'd bought for the chimney into the bucket of his backhoe and raise it up to roof level so that he wouldn't have to lug buckets of bricks up a ladder. Genius, right? He thought so.

While using the backhoe was a surprisingly great idea and just when we thought our hero had redeemed himself brain-cell-wise, we see that he once again allowed Gravel to "help." So, no, sadly Rock is still in the "never learn from one's mistakes" category.

Over one hundred bricks were loaded into the backhoe, along with a bucket of pre-mixed mortar and the assorted tools Rock would need for his masonry feat. He drove the backhoe right up to the house, raised the bucket up to the roof, then climbed the ladder to the roof.

Now Rock had managed to learn one lesson from his previous adventures with the alien child—*do not allow alien onto the roof with you.* To do so is to invite dismemberment, disfigurement and/or death. He was even so conscientious of this fact that he pulled the ladder up on the roof with him so that Gravel was relegated to the ground, a fact which he complained loudly—and long-ly—about.

Rock walked back and forth from the bucket to the chimney, carrying a stack of new bricks to his build site, then taking a stack of the old crumbly bricks back to the backhoe bucket. This was a time-consuming process and Gravel got bored watching his dad walk back and forth.

"I'm gonna go get a sandwich, kay, dad?" he called after Rock's third trip back to the bucket.

"Yeah, whatever," Rock grunted as he hefted another heavy armload.

In the time it took for Gravel to go in the house, find his mom, tell her he wanted a sandwich, have her tell him it wasn't lunch time yet, then going into the kitchen by himself and fixing a peanut butter and mayonnaise sandwich (yeah, I know, I threw up in my mouth a little just writing that), and then head back outside, his dad had finally finished moving the bricks and was contemplating yet again the design of the new chimney—like a rectangular brick roof fixture is some great architectural feat.

The eating of the sandwich diversion lasted all of five minutes before Gravel was once again bored. He climbed up on the shovel part of the backhoe and sat swinging his legs back and forth and back and forth, bored to tears. It had been a whole twenty minutes since he and his dad had come outside, after all. Twenty long, borrrrrrrring minutes.

A little appliance-sized bulb went off over the child's head at that moment. If the bucket of the backhoe reached the roof, maybe the shovel could too! Then he could surprise his dad and maybe get to help. Maybe he might even get to lay some bricks...then he could tell his little sister, Pebbles, that *he* got to work on the chimney for Santa and that maybe *he* would get extra presents. That would for sure make her cry. And that would be awesome!

So with thoughts of breaking his sister's heart warming him, Gravel jumped off the shovel and climbed into the driver's seat of the backhoe.

There were so many levers and buttons and knobs that Gravel was briefly intimidated, but that feeling quickly left him when he noticed his dad had left the keys in the ignition. Score!

Even ten-year-olds know that getting any sort of vehicle to do what you want starts with turning the key. So that's what he did. The problem was... well, there were a whole lot of problems, so let's start that over. Here is the list of what was wrong with this situation:

One, the old backhoe didn't have the safety features that the newer models do, so when you started one without putting the clutch in, it would lurch forward (or backward, if you left it in reverse, duh);

Two, at that very moment, Rock had returned to the backhoe's bucket and climbed in to retrieve his mortar;

Three, when the backhoe lurched forward, it hit the house and jerked Rock forward and then back, causing him to do a sort of helicopter spinning thing with his arms, which caused him to land inside the bucket; and

Four, Gravel panicked over the lurching machine and jumped off the seat, but not before he snagged the bucket tilt lever with his jacket.

Did you know that when you tilt a backhoe bucket with a two-hundred-fifty-pound dude and five hundred pounds of bricks in it, that the man will fall first to the ground? Aye, 'tis true. I'm not sure what physics law this is, but I think it's probably more like a Murphy's Law. Or a Loony Toons Law.

So when the man falls to the ground first, that means that the bricks will follow. And every last one of them will manage to hit the man. Every. Last. One.

And let's not forget about the bucket of mortar.

Result: Yet another concussion; a broken wrist, nose and foot; numerous brick-sized bruises and cuts; large bald spots where dried mortar had to be chiseled out of hair; one alien child who wisely went into hiding.

Superman Never Had Children

Rock was a mechanic. I probably forgot to mention that, huh? Well, he was. He's retired now and that's mostly because of situations like this one.

Our heroish dude guy was under a 1983 Plymouth Horizon reattaching a wire to the starter. It's normally a really simple and quick fix, but of course nothing ever goes as planned. and this particular car was really low to the ground, so Rock just jacked the thing up and didn't bother with safety features like jack stands. I know, he never learns.

Alien child was once again wandering around, bored, and apparently looking for a way to maim and dismember his father. Leaving his dad in the driveway with the car, Gravel shuffled into the garage and over to his dad's workbench. There he found a large metal clamp. He messed with it for a minute, twisting the screw that tightened the clamp and unscrewing it over and over. Then that little appliance bulb went off over his noggin and he moved back to the garage door where he attached the clamp right in the middle.

Well, that didn't last long to entertain him. In thirty seconds he was bored yet again. He bent down to look at his dad under the car.

"Whatcha doin'?" He spit on the ground like he'd seen his dad doing. "Thought we were gonna go to McDonald's." The kid was always hungry. Like three Happy Meals' in one sitting hungry.

Rock grunted. "We will. I just gotta fix this car. It'll just be a minute. Go play, kay?" Rock blew out a breath of frustration. Keeping aliens entertained was full-time work.

The boy was quiet for a minute, so Rock concentrated on what he was doing. He needed to get Mrs. Jackson's car finished so the old lady could get to her bingo game and quit calling him every thirty minutes.

Gravel kicked a few rocks around the yard for a few minutes, but that was ended quickly when one stray rock skipped over to the driveway and hit his dad, who yelled really loud. Scowling, Gravel then wandered back to where his dad was working and that's when he noticed a handle sticking out from under the car. Curiosity and alien-induced trouble-seeking forced his hand to the handle. I'm not sure what told him to turn that handle though.

Turning the handle of course released the jack and brought the car down. On top of Rock.

Despite the fact that he found himself pinned underneath a freaking *car*, and despite the fact that said car had just about crushed his sternum into bone dust *and* squished all the air out of his lungs, Rock had two things going for him: One, it was one of those K cars that were made during the time when car manufacturers were trying to be more environmentally friendly, so the car was pretty lightweight to increase gas mileage. Two, Rock's hands had been above his head at the time while he was reattaching the wire and so he was able to literally push the car off his body. And three (oh, did I say only two things going for him? I meant three), Rock is a big guy and is pretty strong.

In a little bit of a panic and a whole lot of adrenaline rush, Rock practically tossed the car off his chest. Well, he at least pushed it up and then down, off his body.

He then jumped up, ready to fight (adrenaline, remember?) and cracked his skull on the clamp the kid had installed on the garage door.

The stars and birdies floating around his head were pretty, but the blood dripping into his eyes was a bit annoying.

Getting a wad of paper towels and shoving them up into his hat to stop the blood flow, Rock went back out to finish working, knowing he'd have to go into town later to get stitches. To the hospital—he sure as heck wasn't calling Beglenda.

Gravel was once again nowhere to be found (Rock swore the kid had teleporting abilities) and so Rock jacked the car up again (once he was able to get air back into his lungs) and then made sure he removed the jack handle. Safety first and all that. Well, I guess this would be safety second.

He managed to get the car fixed and called Mrs. I Have To Go To Bingo TONIGHT Because My Social Security Check Came In Today Jackson to tell her that her car was operational once again and then decided he needed to look for the boy. Skillet had long before given up on trying to keep track of the child and so, unfortunately, all alien herding responsibility fell entirely on Rock's shoulders. And his shoulders were getting a bit tired, frankly.

Gravel had run into the barn when he thought he'd flattened his father and after a brief period of mourning—probably less than five minutes—he decided that he should cut all the strands on the hay bales, thinking how much more time-efficient feeding the animals would be that way.

Rock groaned when he saw the mess his kid had made. He'd be spending the next three months using a pitchfork and a wheelbarrow to feed the flocks. Back to the eighteen hundreds.

"C'mon," he told Gravel as he pushed him out of the barn, "let's find something you can do that won't cause me pain and suffering."

They were walking near the house when Rock noticed the riding lawn mower. Knowing the kid's penchant for vehicles and things with motors, Rock got the not-so-brilliant-when-he-thought-about-it-later idea to let the kid ride around the three acres surrounding their house on the mower. He would disengage the blades first, of course. He *was* a responsible parent, after all. Sort of.

Gravel was obviously thrilled to be allowed to drive all by himself. He immediately proceeded to drive all over the property. He went all the way down to the cow pasture fence and then around the barn and back up toward the house. He then went around and around the house, going as fast as he possibly could without braking.

During Gravel's impromptu NASCAR training session, Rock, satisfied the boy would be occupied for at least a half hour, went back to his work, which meant replacing the brakes on an old Duster one of his friends' kids drove. He grumbled when the blood from his head wound started dripping into his eyes again and wiped it on his t-shirt. After doing this several times, he happened to glance down at his blood-stained t-shirt. He thought he looked like he'd either cut an artery, or else had been playing an extra in a B-rated horror movie. He hoped no one came by—they might get freaked out by the gore.

Rock was banging on a lug nut that wouldn't come loose when he heard something that ironically made his heart stop and speed up at the same time...a very loud BOOM.

It was the unmistakable sound of a riding lawn mower hitting something large. Not that he'd ever heard a riding lawn mower hit something large, but logic and deduction told him that was exactly what he heard, and he took off running.

Rock had just made it around the house when his wife came running out of the house (with a skillet in hand, her favorite weapon of choice). She saw her husband and yelled, "What the blankety-blank was that?" to which Rock squared his shoulders—he knew of what wrath the woman was capable of—and prepared to tell her that the noise was likely her son embedding himself in the wall of the house.

"Uh, probably a bird?" came out of his mouth instead of the truth.

He glanced at the flames of hell-fire shooting from the woman's eyes and he took off again, running toward the side of the house, trying to find the alien. He shivered as he ran by her, swearing he could feel the heat of her gaze on him. The woman was seriously scary. Like Damien in *The Omen*. Or Regan in *The Exorcist*. Or Carrie in, uh, well, *Carrie*. Like all wrapped up together in one psycho package. He also made a mental note that she didn't even ask about all the blood he had on him, grumbling that she was probably just sorry she wasn't the cause of it.

When he rounded the side of the house, he saw his son lying on the porch and his heart lurched again. He *was* worried the kid was seriously hurt, but self-preservation also kicked in and he started planning an escape to a third world country when mom got there and saw what happened.

Rock leapt over the porch rail and ran over to his son. He carefully turned the kid over and blew out a sigh of relief. He was not only intact, he was laughing.

He helped Gravel sit up, grateful he was alive and apparently unharmed, and said a prayer of thanks that he wouldn't have to pack his bags. But then his hands clenched into fists with the desire to wrap themselves around the alien's neck at his next words.

"That was awesome! Can I do that again?"

Yep. There's no denying the parentage of that one.

Results: Eight staples on the top of his head; a permanent hexagon-shaped indent from the oil pan drain plug embedded in his sternum bone (seriously, you can see it on x-rays); an alien-shaped imprint on the north wall of his house.

Sticky Situation

When Gravel was a bit older, he grew into a rather large boy and was capable of helping Rock around the ranch a lot more. Surprisingly, the trying-to-kill-dad incidents lessened and the two had a pretty good working relationship. For the most part.

But there was always room for improvement. Like the fact that Gravel thought he knew more than his father could ever possibly hope to learn and, in fact, thought his parental figure was rather backwards and stupid. The boy had no qualms about telling his dad exactly what he thought of him (Soap-Box Moment: Mouthy kids are the direct result of lack of discipline—

especially when one parent is terrified of reprisal from the other parent if they so much as say "no" to a kid. But that's another story) and Gravel often just flat-out refused to listen to his old man.

Today's story is one of those times. The two men (well, one was a man and the other was just pretending to be, but we won't judge Rock) were mending fence where the cows, doing what cows do, had once again pushed it down.

Rock is fond of calling himself a "CAB," which stands for Cheap, um, an A word that rhymes with "grass", Bast—uh, a B word that starts with "Bas" and ends with "tard." What that means is Rock is always looking for a good deal and invariably buys whatever is cheapest…which often ends up being total crap. Cheap crap, but crap nonetheless.

Case in point: Rock had gotten a "smoking deal" from the local hardware store on a new type of barb wire that was a third of the price of the regular stuff. The only catch was he had to pre-order it and wait two weeks to get it. At the time, Rock had thought "Score!" but once he picked the wire up, he wasn't too sure about the stuff—it looked cheap and felt flimsy. But hey, it was cheap, right? Sigh.

Barb wire has to be stretched in order to get it tight, so Rock had set up what is known as a "fence stretcher" (I KNOW…what a great name, right?) and tightened it just a little so that he could attach the sharp, poky, deadly wire to the post. It was Gravel's job to operate the stretcher when his dad was ready.

They got the top wire installed easily enough and moved to the second strand. Rock wrapped the wire around the post and stapled it, then told Gravel to start cranking the stretcher.

After three cranks, Rock yelled, "Hold it!" But Gravel, being the know-it-all teen who knows better than any adult, said, "It's still too loose," and proceeded to crank it again.

Rock yelled back, "No, don't! This is cheap Chinese wire. You can't stretch it that far or it'll snap—" and with one more crank on the stretcher whilst completely ignoring his dad, Gravel yelped when the wire snapped. Like his dad had just said it would. Exactly like that.

Fortunately, Gravel managed to jump back just in time to avoid getting torn up by the wire, since he was young and his reflexes were top-notch. Unfortunately, Rock, being that he was heading into the age of squishy middle sections and snow-capped heads, had much slower reflexes. Of course, it also didn't help that at the time it snapped he was watching the wire where it was attached to the post and didn't realize he was in the path of a recoiling barbed snake.

Later, Rock realized the strange "PING" he'd heard in that moment that sounded like a banjo being played by a caffeinated raccoon wearing mittens, was, in fact, twenty feet of angry, razor-sharp wire being released from its confines like a rabid Doberman snapping its chain and charging for the neighbor's cat.

The wire was on him before Rock could even register what was happening and before he could even scream—or at least tell Gravel that he was a stubborn idiot—it whipped around him, swallowing him like a tornado in an east Texas mobile home park.

Once again, Gravel took off…this time, in Rock's truck. With Rock's cell phone. And his wire cutters.

Results: One half-finished fence; one shredded Rock; one cool new tattoo on his arm to cover up the scar left behind from cheap Chinese barb wire.

Chapter 4 ANIMALS ARE FOOD, NOT FRIENDS

(WARNING: Animals die in this chapter. Most from being hunted. Some from accidents. A few from laughing too hard at our hero)

Coffee Breaks Are Not For Hunting

When Rock was a bit older (but not wiser…no, never that), he managed a tire store slash auto repair shop. True to his good ol' boy nature, Rock had naturally hired some of the locals who were of the same mindset as he. Which makes sense if they're business-minded, responsible type guys. But it makes zero, zilch, nada, nope, none, no sense if they're of the redneck, backwoods, hillbilly persuasion, because more than one of those types in the kitchen is always a recipe for disaster.

Granted, Rock was trying really hard by this point to be the upstanding manager-type-of-a-guy he thought he should be. I mean, he even did payroll, for Pete's sake. And on time, even! He also wanted to be a good role model for the younger guys who worked for him and so he did his best to act managerlyish. But as with everything in this world, the bad always brings the good down and not the other way around.

One day after a snowstorm, the shop was pretty quiet. Business had slowed to a crawl and the guys had so far only managed to install one set of snow tires and fixed the dent in Mrs. Lewis's Honda where she'd slid into the corner of the sheriff's station on the ice. She was too embarrassed to have Sheriff Rogers find out she was the one who knocked that brick off his building—after all, she and Mrs. Rogers were on the hospitality committee together at the Baptist church—and so she'd wanted the evidence of her "crime" covered up. Literally.

When there isn't something to keep them busy, the boys in the shop would get bored—and in trouble—quicker than a fox running from an old lady with a shotgun (but that's another upcoming story). Rock always gave them busy work, but that only lasted so long…and then the trouble would start.

On this particular day, Rock was in the office doing paperwork, aka taking a nap, when he suddenly noticed that the shop was quiet. Too quiet. And just like when the parent of a toddler suddenly realizes they haven't heard their child in awhile and they just *know* something has been painted, cut, broken, or maimed, Rock burst out of his office and ran into the shop.

It was empty. Not a soul in sight. This was not good. Well, maybe it was good, actually, because if they weren't in the shop, then they weren't making a mess in an area he cared about, except for...*Crap!*

Rock threw open the back door and looked out into the parking lot. Sure enough, there the moe-rons were, all huddled up around the Cheetah (which is a rapid tire inflator), giggling like little girls. Rock was almost afraid to find out what they were doing.

Now just so y'all know, the rapid tire inflator is designed to expel a significant amount of air in a split second. Like a blast. It's a lot of pressure and a lot of power. It could be a dangerous piece of equipment, especially in the wrong hands; which, as we know, was the case here.

Before Rock could take one step out of the door, the Cheetah went off with a "BOOM" that would have made the bomb squad team dive for cover. Rock looked up into the sky to see what exactly the boys had launched. It looked like a duct tape ball with a little bit of red sticking out of the top, the color of a shop rag.

With a bit of unease mixed with excitement, Rock watched the path of the projectile. It was heading to the small, partially frozen pond in the field at the back of the property. The pond where ducks, rabbits and other assorted wildlife often went.

Sure enough, the moe-rons were aiming at the pond, and in particular, the ducks. Surprisingly, they managed to actually hit one of the ducks, who took the duct tape ball in the head, knocking him onto his side, just like one of those metal ducks at the shooting gallery. Only this duck didn't pop back up.

Fists pumped the air and a round of cheers went up, followed by a quick "shhhh!" Rock smirked, knowing they were trying not to get caught in their little escapade.

"Too late," he announced as he walked up to the group. Twelve extra-wide eyeballs stared back at him then and he noticed that while some faces reddened, others paled. He figured most of the guys were afraid they were going to be sent to the firing squad.

He decided to let the guys off the hook. "Nice shootin', Tex," he drawled to Bill, who was manning the Cheetah. "What else have you shot?"

A collective sigh of relief went through the group then when they realized their boss wasn't ticked off. Or planning on dragging them in front of the "firing squad"—figuratively, or literally.

"So far we got two ducks, a pheasant and a rabbit," Jimmy, otherwise known as "Big Foot" because of his size and hairiness, answered. He was usually the leader of the group when they got into trouble.

Rock laughed a little, but then a thought entered his mind and he frowned at them. "Uh, you guys got hunting licenses? And it ain't duck season, is it? Or rabbit...and what else did you say?"

Jimmy stood then and put his hands up. "Pheasant. Now, boss, we ain't *really* huntin'. I mean, we ain't usin' guns or bows, right? We figured that we could just say we was testin' our air compressor and it ain't our fault the stupid animals got in the way."

Well, now, that excuse actually sounded pretty reasonable to Rock (I did say he was *trying* to be upstanding; I didn't say he'd actually managed to get to that point), so he just told the guys to make sure they collected all the evidence at the scene of their crime and he went back in to nap…uh, work.

He was halfway through a rather nice nap—uh, paperwork session—when he heard yelling and doors slamming and then heard one of the bay doors open and then close again. He got up to see what was going on and stopped in disbelief in the shop doorway.

It took a full minute to process the scene: There was a trail of blood on the garage floor that looked like a bucket of pain had been spilled; the trail led to the back of the shop, behind the tire rack; the moe-rons were running all over the place, some putting the Cheetah back in place and others were frantically wiping up the blood and sprinkling cat litter on it; and Jimmy was hauling the mop bucket out of the cleaning closet.

Rock cursed loudly enough to be heard. "What in the hay-ell did you do now?" His booming voice echoed off the steel bay doors.

All movement stopped as once again twelve wide eyeballs looked at him with fear and dread. Rock stomped into the shop and pointed at the cat litter soaking up the blood.

"Who died?"

Jimmy stepped forward again, probably realizing none of the others were brave enough to face the wrath of Rock—he was just downright scary when he was ticked off. Apparently, Rock had been taking psycho lessons from his wife. And Jimmy was the only one big enough to stand up to the boss, a guy who had grown to immense proportions himself.

Jimmy cleared his throat. "Um, well, see, we thought that since the wheel weights in the shop towel worked so good, we'd try something heavier, like an oil filter, to make it maybe go farther. Uh, and hit something bigger..."

Rock crossed his arms and pinched his nose between his thumb and forefinger as he closed his eyes as if in pain. And he *was* in pain, knowing what was coming next.

"And did it work?" he asked without looking up, almost afraid of the answer.

Jimmy grinned and nodded, before realizing his boss couldn't see that. "Yeah, it worked real good."

Rock sighed heavily and began rubbing his forehead. "And what exactly did it work on?"

"Oh, you mean what did we hit? Uh, we killed a deer."

That comment brought Rock's head up. "A deer?" he yelled and looked around at the others.

"You morons! Deer season ended over two weeks ago!"

Jimmy cocked his head to the side. "But you didn't have a problem with it when we were shootin' ducks."

Rock shook his head. "Ducks is one thing. The season is still open and that's just a fine for huntin' without a license."

Gravel, who Rock had hired in a moment of sheer stupidity, stepped up then.

"But it ain't huntin' if we don't use guns, right?"

Rock turned his fiery gaze on his loins issue. "No, son, it ain't huntin'. It's out of season, so that means it's poachin'. And it also seems like cheatin'."

Jimmy grinned then. "Cheatin' with the Cheetah."

Rock frowned at him, a silent warning to shut the heck up. He pointed a finger at the group.

"You all better be danged thankful the game warden wasn't around..."

His voice trailed off when he noticed the twelve eyeballs were all wide again and Adams apples were bobbing. Rock cursed.

"Lemme guess—Frank was in the area, right?"

Jimmy cleared his throat again. "Uh, yeah, he was, uh, in the drive-thru at Sonic."

The Sonic Drive-In shared a side of the parking lot with Rock's shop and anyone who happened to be in the drive-thru had a very good view of the back of the shop...and the parking lot. And the impromptu hunting.

Rock cursed again, more colorfully this time. He pointed a finger at the idiots again.

"You all better be kissing your lucky whatevers that Frank didn't see you..."

Once again, his voice trailed off at the look on everyone's faces, that had all gone from pale to bright red.

"Are you kidding me? He *saw* you hit that deer?"

Gravel spoke up again. "No, dad, don't worry. He didn't see us hit the deer."

"Oh, thank God," Rock mumbled as he released a weary breath, trying to get his blood pressure back down under a thousand over a million.

"But he did see us draggin' the deer back to the shop."

Before Rock could wrap his big ol' bear paws around Gravel's neck, the alarm on the front door sounded, alerting them to the fact that someone had entered the shop. Rock turned in the direction of the door and could see that it was, in fact, Frank. The local game warden.

Rock turned back around to tell the morons that they had better tell the warden the truth about what happened, but there wasn't a single one to be found. They'd all managed to disappear in a split second. Apparently, Gravel had taught them all teleportation techniques.

Thankfully, Frank was a pretty good friend of Rock's and Rock had just given the guy a great deal on snow tires for his personal vehicle the week before, so Frank was inclined to go easy on him.

Rock had tried to argue that it was the guys who had committed the crime and that Frank should go after them—at that point Rock was more than happy to throw them all under the bus—but the warden had insisted that since it was Rock's shop and property, as well as Rock's employees, Rock was responsible for all the fines and fees. Of course, that actually translated to: "You're the one with the money. The boys would all just get community service."

Results: One freezer full of venison, duck, pheasant and rabbit (Rock claimed he had more than paid for all that meat, regardless of who did the killing, and if the boys didn't want to end up in his freezer too, they'd all shut up about it); one bank account seven hundred and fifty-five dollars lighter; one expensive new lock and chain on the Cheetah.

Old Picasso Had A Farm

Once the guys discovered the launching capabilities of the Cheetah, sending various items into the stratosphere became the new game...whenever

Rock let them use it, that is.

Rock didn't want to get into more trouble with the State of Colorado (and he sure as heck didn't want to give them more of his hard-earned money), so he moved Operation Cheating Cheetah (Jimmy insisted on the name) to his home base, which was also where his personal auto shop was located. At least then they'd be on private property and away from governmental eyes.

The guys set the Cheetah up in the large parking area between Rock's house and auto shop and aimed it at the cow pasture. At least that way they wouldn't be hitting anything expensive.

The first item to go into the Cheetah was tennis balls. They went pretty far, but they weren't very exciting. Just bounced a few times in the field before getting lost in the tall grass. Big deal.

Next was oranges. Not a good idea, because they tend to disintegrate when they come out of the tube and leave behind a sticky mess. They also coat everyone nearby with orange juice. Apples weren't much better, although the applesauce they made was pretty good.

"This ain't no juicer," Rock growled. "We need to find something better to shoot."

"Yeah, like some blasting caps," Gravel supplied with a grin. He lost his smile and backed up a step when he saw the look his father gave him.

"How 'bout some ball bearings?" Bill, aka "Who's Your Daddy?" offered.

Rock shook his head in a moment of adultness. "Nah, too destructive." But then one of those light bulb thingies went off over his head.

"Not ball bearings, but paintballs!"

"Yeah," Gravel added, excited that his dad wasn't going to nix the whole operation, "and glow sticks!"

With a round of approval, the group rushed to the truck so they could head to town to buy the needed supplies.

Two hours later—encompassing one shopping trip to Wally World for paintballs, glow sticks and, as a last minute thought, frozen Cornish hens; a stop at Mickey D's for food since Gravel couldn't go more than two hours without filling his craw; a fuel stop with Rock grumbling that he was having to foot the entire bill for the supplies, food, *plus* diesel for his truck; then a stop at one of Bill's ex's so he could drop off a child support payment—the group made their way back to Rock's ranch.

The Cornish hens were the first to go into the tube. It was a tight fit, since the extension on the Cheetah was only three inches in diameter, but using a stick and a hammer, they managed to get the first one installed.

"Crank it up to one fifty!" Gravel told his dad once he aimed the tube toward the dog's pen. The idea was that they would get to launch a mini-chicken *and* feed the dogs at the same time. Win-win.

Rock shook his head. "Too high," he said, but gave in when the group gave him a round of boos and "party pooper" comments. So to one hundred fifty PSI it went.

Did you know that when you shove a partially thawed four-inch mini-chicken into a three-inch diameter tube with a stick and a hammer, then shoot said mini-chicken forty feet into the air with one hundred fifty pounds per square inch of air pressure, the poor little mini-chicken becomes chicken nuggets?

The dogs didn't care what form their dinner came in. They loved chicken—Cornish or regular-sized, raw or cooked, or even still running around the coop squawking and flapping. It was pretty much all the same to them. So when chicken nuggets started raining down on their heads, they thought the Lord had offered manna from Heaven.

So after shooting the other three Cornish hens to the dogs, the guys decided to move on to the glow sticks. They spent a good twenty minutes bending the three hundred sticks and shaking them to get the glow started and then another argument ensued about just how much pressure they should crank that baby up to. Rock thought one fifty was plenty; Gravel wanted to go at least to one eighty, which was the top limit of the safety zone; Jimmy and Bill voted for two hundred.

Two hundred it was. This time, Rock got to do the honors of slamming the lever to release the pressure while Gravel insisted on doing a countdown.

BOOM! The decibel level of the explosion coming from the Cheetah was equivalent to a mine operation blowing the side of a mountain off. Or a nuclear explosion. Or an alien infant screaming for his mama.

Since it was nearing dusk and not quite dark yet, the glow sticks weren't very visible as they left earth's atmosphere. The guys thought that was a really disappointing launch, since they didn't get to see where the darned things would land.

Oh well, on to the best part—the arsenal of two cans of two thousand paintballs, multi-color, no less. The guys spared no expense of Rock's money.

They learned their lesson not to crank the Cheetah up so high if they had any hopes of seeing where the paintballs would land, so Jimmy turned the PSI down to a reasonable one fifty. Bill poured the balls into the tube.

"Five, four, three, two...ONE!" Gravel yelled as he slammed the lever down and another BOOM sounded, still loud but less obnoxious than the last one. But honestly, a rocket launcher would have been less obnoxious.

Success! The paintballs exited the tube with enough velocity to promise a good distance, but not so much that they ended up in orbit around the earth.

But...and here's the big butt, uh but...right at about the time Gravel pulled the lever, he also kicked his foot out, I guess in a pitcher throwing a baseball type of maneuver, and he bumped the tube. Not enough to knock it over, but it was enough to tilt it...straight overhead.

The guys realized what had happened about two seconds before the cloud of paint-filled projectiles started their descent back down (darned ol' Newton...again). Everyone ran in a different direction, but they all ran into each other in true comedic fashion first before scrambling away.

Rock dove under his wife's bus—she drove for the local school system, and how someone with absolutely no patience or even a tolerance for children could do that is beyond comprehension, but digression has occurred again—and Gravel headed for the tractor. Jimmy, being that he was roughly the size of a defensive lineman standing on the shoulders of an offensive lineman and wouldn't fit underneath anything in the yard, ran for the workshop with Bill following close behind.

The sound of four thousand paintballs hitting the ground was pretty impressive and surprisingly—or maybe not so surprising—it went on for what seemed like ten minutes. It was probably more like thirty seconds, but when you're hiding like a sissy la la girl, time seems to drag on.

Finally, the rainstorm of painted death balls stopped and the guys came out of hiding and looked around at the results of their launch. Almost immediately, Rock wanted to head back under the bus and stay there until his wife came out the next morning and ran him over. Because once she saw what he and the boys had done, he was a dead man anyway. At least death by a thirteen ton vehicle was preferable to some of the more clever things the wife could think up.

The area looked like a scene from a Dr. Seuss book. There were lovely round blotches in all the colors of the rainbow as far as the eye could see. Over every square foot of Rock's ranch. "Oh my gawwwd, when the wife sees this, we're dead" polka dots of covered the grass, the lawn mower, the barn, the workshop, the house, the tractor, the cars…and yes, the wife's school bus. The bus she insisted be kept in pristine condition at all times.

Jimmy stood beside Rock and just breathed heavily, apparently understanding the overwhelming gravity of the situation. Only his best friend would get it—Jimmy had been his best man, for Pete's sake, so he knew the wife just about as well as Rock did. He also knew exactly what she was capable of when angered.

His best friend wrapped a comforting arm around Rock's shoulder and sighed. Rock waited, knowing Jimmy would have some great advice, pearls of wisdom.

"Well," Jimmy said, "sucks to be you. See ya." And with that, the coward yelled to Bill since they had come to the ranch together, and the two of them ran for his truck like their tails were on fire and their heads were a'catchin' and peeled out down the driveway.

One thing Rock had going for him was the fact that his wife and Pebbles had gone shopping in a town about three hours away…and the sky was dark and it smelled like rain. There was hope.

Gravel walked up to his dad then. "Think it'll rain and clean all this mess up, dad? Cuz if Mom sees this…" he didn't finish the sentence, but just shuddered.

"If the good Lord is merciful, it will rain," Rock replied, trying to sound hopeful. He had no doubts God *could* make it rain, but *would* He? Well, that was a million dollar question. *Probably not. Her seeing this mess is gonna be my punishment…like bein' married to her ain't enough, Lord!*

Shaking his head at his thoughts, Rock walked toward the workshop to get the spray washer. If he at least washed her bus, maybe she wouldn't try to throw him under it.

By the time Rock walked out of the workshop, it had started to sprinkle. By the time he set the spray washer up, it had started raining in earnest.

Gravel was celebrating in the driveway, doing a sort of maniacal rain dance. It looked like a combination of the chicken dance and an actual chicken getting electrocuted. Gravel had a good reason to be happy knowing that he, too, would be in his mom's sights for the polka dot landscape. The rain washing the evidence away was truly a reason to celebrate.

"You're supposed to do the dance *before* it rains," Rock yelled at him.

The guys put all the eviden—uh, stuff they had out away, and went into the house to change out of their wet clothes. They met back in the living room and celebrated their good fortune by watching "South Park."

Kenny had just died when the wife and Pebbles came home.

"What the (insert four letter word here) did you do today?" were the first words out of her mouth as she tossed her purse and packages on the dining table.

Rock and Gravel looked at each other in horror. *What does she mean?* Gravel mouthed with wide, frantic eyes. *Didn't the rain wash it all away?*

I don't know! Rock mouthed back. He assumed it had, but since it had been pouring by the time they put the Cheetah away, they'd run for the house and hadn't gone back out since.

"Would you two morons stop mouthing at each other and answer my question?" Skillet came around to the front of the couch to face them and crossed her arms over her rather ample bosom while she scowled.

Without waiting for them to form an answer, she continued, "Mom called my cell when we were at Macy's and said Mrs. Jackson called her to tell her that the aliens had crapped all over her front lawn." She rolled her eyes.

"And you know my mom…anything alien or ghost related and she's on it. So the woman rushed over there, only to find about three hundred glow sticks all over Mrs. Jackson's property."

The wife pointed her freshly manicured finger at Rock. "Mom knew right then it had to be you and the other morons—" she moved her finger to Gravel then, "—and called me to rat you out. So now tell me, what the (insert the same or different four letter word here) did you do?"

Rock sighed, mostly from relief that she wasn't asking about the paintballs. But the sigh also included a bit of resignation over the fact that he knew he was still going to get chewed out.

"We were just messin' around. Didn't mean no harm," he started.

"Yeah," Gravel added when he saw his mother move her hands to her hips, a sure sign she was about to really let go with a lecture that would mostly consist of yelling at jet engine decibels. "We just launched some stuff in the air."

Rock groaned softly at his son's not-helpful words. *Here it comes…*

Those beady eyes narrowed even further. "And exactly what other 'stuff' did you launch?"

Gravel swallowed audibly and shot a frantic look at his dad. "Uh, nothing major, Ma. Just some fruit, apples and oranges. They made a mess."

He grinned then.

"And we fed the dogs by shooting chicken at them."

The beady eyes turned to Rock then and he could swear he saw the fires of hell burning in them once again.

"Chicken? Are you saying you used the chicken I had thawing in the fridge for dinner?" Her voice was so low, Rock thought it sounded like a grizzly.

"No!" Gravel answered quickly before Rock could. "We bought some of those little chickens. You know, the ones that you made for that fancy dinner you had a couple of weeks ago."

She turned back to Rock and narrowed her eyes even further. He thought for sure, between her scowl and the snarl on her mouth, her newly plucked eyebrows were going to mate with her upper lip.

"Cornish hens? You fed the dogs four-dollar-a-pound *Cornish hens?*"

Gravel apparently wasn't born with that gene that tells you when imminent danger is brewing and warns you to back pedal. Rock covered his face with his hand while his son nodded enthusiastically.

"Yeah! It was so awesome too…the chickens just sort of exploded over the pen. You shoulda seen the dogs—they were like, 'woohoo! Chicken nuggets from the sky!'"

She was quiet for a moment and Rock chanced a look at her through his fingers. She was looking back at him with a "he's *your* child" look. He shrugged. No sense arguing.

He sighed. "We launched the glow sticks and didn't mean for them to go so high," Rock tried to explain.

"We had no idea where they would land."

Skillet harrumphed and turned back to collect her packages. "Well, you better just count your lucky stars they didn't land *here*," she said as she picked up her numerous bags.

Gravel started to say something and Rock elbowed him in the ribs… hard.

"Ouch! What'd you do that for?" he complained as he rubbed his side. Rock looked at his wife to see if she'd heard their less-than-bright son's comment, but like a cougar climbing a mountain with a juicy rabbit, she had headed upstairs with the day's kill.

So it seemed they had gotten away with Operation Cheating Cheetah with very little repercussions, other than Skillet knowing they had launched some "stuff" and Mrs. Jackson thinking aliens were crapping in her yard. Thankfully, the paintball fiasco had been nicely washed away.

The next morning when Rock was up just before dawn and went out on his back porch to drink his coffee before starting the day's chores, as he did every day. In the pasture just behind the house, the cows and sheep were happily grazing on the soft prairie grass that had sprung up over the summer. The nights had gotten cool enough for them to move into the barns and sheep enclosure, but as soon as the sun started to appear, the animals would head out to graze.

As the sun peaked over the mountain to the east of the ranch, the sight that met Rock caused him to choke on his coffee and blew some out of his nose (which hurts a lot, by the way).

It was then that he realized his thought of getting away with Operation Cheating Cheetah was completely and utterly wrong, because there was no way to hide this evidence. Or even clean it up. He was royally screwed.

Every cow and every sheep had rainbow polka dots.

Results: Mrs. Jackson's status as the county's craziest lady was firmly established; Skillet confiscated the Cheetah (which just meant Rock had to buy another one); the Dr. Seuss sheep and cows became a state attraction.

It Go Boom

Then there was that time…

Rock's father-in-law du jour Dusty (Beglenda traded husbands more often than most people traded cars) had asked for help clearing some trees from where he wanted to put a new pasture, since his herd had grown by several hundred head. Rock, of course, volunteered, since he loved getting away from his own small ranch (Read: getting away from Skillet).

Dusty had hired a live-in ranch hand named, surprisingly, Cowboy. Cowboy came with the added bonus of a teenaged son named Albert and father and son could out-work a whole crew of men on any given day. Rock kept threatening to steal the pair away from Dusty to work in his tire store.

Gravel had gone with his dad to help at the big ranch (and to also get away from Skillet), as had Pebbles, who was planning to spend the weekend helping her Grandma Beglenda sort through her "alien abduction evidence," which mostly consisted of grocery store rag magazine clippings with stories from drunken hillbillies claiming they were abducted (most likely to have an excuse for not coming home for three days when they'd gone on a bender).

Gravel apparently had decided he did not want to be outdone by fellow teen Albert, so he'd worked harder than Rock had ever seen the boy work. The two teens seemed to have an unspoken competition going and were felling trees left and right, to the point that the older men stopped working and just watched.

Dusty hocked a big loogie before drawling, "If I'd known that's all it'd take to get them boys to work like that, I woulda gotten them together a lot sooner."

In no time at all, the clearing was a clearing (to the point that Dusty, Rock and Cowboy had had to yell at the boys "That's enough!" before the were accused of deforestation) and they were just left with stumps to get out. Dusty had brought his John Deere up from the barn and with a chain they were able to pull almost all the stumps out of the ground. Of course, with every stump that came out, a round of cheers had to go up, along with a few manly grunts and Tim the Toolman Taylor styled "arrr arrrr arrrr's."

A few of the larger stumps had to be dug out, but with Gravel and Albert once again competing, that didn't take much time and soon all that was left was a four-foot-diameter stump. It was a doozy, big enough to make a coffee table out of. There was no pulling or digging that sucker out. Rock suggested just leaving the stump in the field to use as a workbench, or a table, or even a small bed, but it was right in the center of the pasture and Dusty just raised an eyebrow in response. The look said, "Are you an idiot?"

The guys stood around in guy-fashion, picking noses and scratching crotches, while they contemplated their options. Everyone gave an opinion and threw crazy ideas around and shot each other down.

"We could maybe chop it up into smaller pieces," Rock suggested. "Be easier to get out that way."

"No," Dusty argued with a roll of his eyes. "You'd still have the roots, boy. I need them out too, 'else the Deere's gonna hang up on them when I plow."

"Could maybe light 'er on fire," Cowboy suggested as he spit a pint of tobacco juice at his feet.

"A good soakin' with some kerosene oughtta do the trick."

Now while the other men (and boys) were enamored with the idea of fire, they quickly nixed the idea due to the fact that it would be a pretty big blaze and the chance of starting a forest fire was too great. It had been a really mild winter and so far spring wasn't looking too good for moisture, either. The entire county was being really cautious with any open flame. It would only take one spark and all the ranchers in the area would be ruined. Sometimes the guys were actually responsible and used the lump two to three feet above their butts. I know; it's shocking.

But the fire idea led to another: "How 'bout we blow it up?" Gravel suggested. All the guys thought that would be a great idea (I mean, most guys are pyromaniacs at heart, but men and explosives? They get down-right giddy over making things "go boom."), but again, there was the fear of fire.

Rock was quiet for a minute and then that dim light bulb went off. "We don't gotta worry' bout fire if we use C4," he suggested.

All the other guys turned and looked at him with the same "Are you stupid?" look on their faces. Dusty, of course, wasn't afraid to speak his mind.

"Are you stupid?" he asked. "Just where the hay-ell do you think we're gonna get C4?"

Rock hesitated a second. "Welllll," he drawled carefully, "I know a guy…"

And he did. KC, his friend from back in the day when they were just kids and doing stupid things like jumping cars with bikes and Tarzan swinging through trees, worked in the supply department at the local military base.

Some government brain donor had put KC in charge of watching their stuff. Apparently they missed the part in his background check where he did a two-year stint in juvie for robbing a convenience store when he was fourteen. And how, while in juvie, he ran a black market commissary out of his dorm. And now he was put in charge of military supplies. Your brilliant government in action, folks.

Anyway, Rock and KC had managed to keep in touch and in fact, the two had just met for beers the week before to discuss such distressing topics as angry, bitter wives (Rock) and receding hair lines (KC). KC had said at the time that if Rock needed something the government might have, to let him know: "Stuff 'goes missing' all the time wink wink." (KC didn't say "wink wink", he actually winked. Just so you know, in case there was confusion.)

Rock though it was possible that KC could maybe get his hands on a little C4, just enough to blow up the stump. It would definitely solve their problem—Rock would be the hero of the day, Dusty might actually finally start liking him, and maybe if he made her mother's husband happy, Skillet might even be nice to him. Not likely, but it was a dream.

After Rock told the guys he'd get back in touch with them if and when he could get some slightly illegal-to-possess explosives, they all went their separate ways. Rock headed straight into town and called KC from a pay phone…just in case the government could or would track phone calls made to a supply department.

"Sergeant Wilcox," KC's voice said. It took Rock a second to realize that KC was, in fact, Sergeant Wilcox.

"Hey KC," he said. "It's me." He hoped KC would know who "me" was, because Rock didn't want to give any incriminating information over the phone. There was dead silence on the other end, so he tried to explain further without giving too much away.

"Uh, you know when we met last week for beers and you said if there was ever anything I needed to, uh, let you know, cuz you might be able to, uh, get it?"

"Oh, hey, Rock!"

Rock cringed at the use of his name. He had hoped his longtime friend would be smarter than that. But no, of course he wasn't.

"Hey. So, uh, I need like some, uh…" he looked around to make sure no one was eavesdropping on his public phone conversation. "…C4," Rock finished the last in a whisper.

"C4?" KC practically yelled into the phone and Rock held the phone to his chest, trying to block the sound coming from it. Rock could just picture the powers-that-be listening in on the other line, furiously scribbling notes…*Rock, need last name. Can't be that many men named Rock. Needs C4. Has connection to Sgt Wilcox.* Oh yeah, he was a cooked goose.

"Uh, never mind, KC," Rock said nervously. "Forget I asked. I only needed a little to get rid of a tree stump." He added the last bit for whoever might be listening…*Nothin' to take note of here, folks. Just a redneck tryin' to do things the easy way. Nothin' nef…nefar…dang it, what's that word? Nothin' bad goin' on here…*

"No, no," KC cut into his thoughts. "Just surprised me, is all. It isn't a big deal, really. I can get you what you need." He lowered his voice then.

"Stuff 'falls off the supply truck' all the time. Know what I mean?"

Rock laughed nervously. "Nervously" seemed to be his adverb for the day. He impressed himself by knowing that it was an adverb, but then second-guessed himself and started thinking about adjectives and prepositions and…

"How much you looking for?" KC asked, once again cutting into his thoughts.

That was a question he didn't really have an answer for. It *was* a big stump and he'd never used C4 before. He'd heard it was pretty powerful stuff, but how much did he need to blow a four foot wide stump into kindling?

"Um, I don't know. Like a pound?" he guessed.

KC made a "hmmm" sound. Rock was hoping he had some C4 chart on his desk, one that had calculations like: "Blowing up enemy base = 1000 pounds; Destroying aircraft carrier = 2800 pounds; Turning tree stump into matchsticks = 1 pound."

Rock could hear what sounded like typing on a keyboard, then KC finally responded. "A pound. Uh, okay. Well, they come in one point two five pound bricks and yeah, I guess I can do that. You need a detonator too?"

"Uh, yeah, I guess so." Rock was starting to worry a little. This was out of his knowledge base and comfort zone.

"Okay, I'll meet you tonight after work at Billy's Bar. Eighteen hundred hours."

Tonight, well, that was fast. He'd expected it to take like a week or so for the stuff to "fall off the truck"…or however it was that KC acquired it.

"Uh, so eighteen hundred—"

"Six o'clock," KC supplied.

Two days later, the guys were all back at the stump and Rock and Cowboy were drilling holes into the top of it so they could pack it with the explosives. Rock stopped working for a minute and looked around, noting that Gravel and Albert were suspiciously absent, so Dusty went looking for them. Before long, he came back to the stump with the two teens in tow.

"The idiots were making sculptures outta the explosives," he announced as he nodded to his hands that were filled with all sorts of little figures. There were trees and animals and what looked like a miniature space shuttle.

Dusty snorted. "Not bad, though. I think Albert might have a real talent for it."

Once the stump holes all had a C4 figurine packed into them, the guys took safety precautions and moved their vehicles back about fifty yards. Dusty, however, wasn't taking any chances with his two-month old Chevy Silverado four-wheel drive quad cab—the danged thing had cost more than his house was worth, for cryin' out loud—and he moved back sixty yards.

Rock poked the wires into the little sculptures and then unrolled the wire spool back to the vehicles, where the detonator was. After making sure everyone was either in a vehicle, or behind one, with Gravel insisting on doing a countdown, Rock set the detonator off.

The blast that sounded literally shook the ground. Rock was a little dazed from the percussion and figured the others were too, since no one said a word.

But then it started to rain wood. Splinters. Slivers. Chunks. Sticks. Sawdust. Rock and Gravel—the only two not inside a vehicle, go figure, like father like son—ran for cover under a nearby tree.

It seemed to shower tree parts for a good ten minutes. It might very well have been ten minutes, considering the size of the stump and the fact that the moe-rons had used an entire package of C4 in a four-foot diameter hunk of wood—an amount of explosive that would be enough to blow all the doors, windows and roof out of a large passenger van.

After the shrapnel finally stopped falling, Rock and Gravel stepped out from under the tree and started to head over to check on the stump. But a clearing of the throat caused them to look back to where Dusty had parked his new pride and joy.

Sticking out of the hissing radiator of that pride and joy was a three-foot long piece of wood. It was horrifying and Rock's first thought was he sure was glad everyone had taken cover before the blast.

But his second thought was that Dusty was looking at him like he was the biggest moe-ron on the planet. At that moment, Rock thought he might just be right.

Results: One tree stump blown to smithereens, whatever "smithereens" is; one lovely Chevy Silverado needing a new grill, radiator, AC condenser, cooling fan, water pump and belts; one very angry father-in-law.

This Is What Happens When Dumb Leads Dumber

One year the whitetail deer had managed to overpopulate themselves in the eastern plains and so the State had opened a special hunting season before the overabundance of animals messed up the whole eco system. It's amazing how such cute furry creatures are capable of destroying life as we know it.

Anyway, it was during this special hunting season that Dusty had asked Rock to come to the big ranch in eastern Colorado and help him take some cattle to Dodge City to sell. Rock had decided to make a mini vacation out of it and headed up a few days early for some rest and relaxation. He should have known better.

Dusty and Rock were out riding through the pastures, making sure the cows weren't doing anything uncowly, when a herd of deer bolted across the field in front of them.

"Man," Dusty whistled, "them deer are thick this year, ain't they?"

Rock agreed. "Yeah, sure are. Big mothers too. You get your tag?"

Dusty hocked a giant tobacco loogie before answering. "Yep, my landowner's. But I ain't hunted yet cuz I don't got no room in the freezer."

Rock rubbed his face with his hand. "Well, ya know it's gettin' down in the teens at night and not much above forty durin' the day. We could just put the meat in a cooler outside. Should keep."

Dusty rubbed his face like Rock had and spit another blob of tobacco juice over the side of the horse.

"Yeah, might work. I got a metal locker we could use. Think that would work more like a freezer."

Rock nodded. "I got my tag and Gravel's got his."

Another loogie hit the ground. "Ya know," Dusty started, "seems to me that it ain't too sportin' to shoot 'em. Be like pickin' off fish in a barrel, ya know? Too danged many of'em. I'm thinkin' we need to make it a little harder. More challengin'."

Rock frowned at his father-in-law. "Whatchu talkin' 'bout?"

Dusty grinned back at him, a lopsided, tobacco stained mouth full of brown teeth showing.

"I'm thinkin' we gotta do it 'Injun Style'."

"What the heck is that?" Rock wasn't too sure he liked the sound of that. It sounded…complicated. And potentially dangerous. And most likely would end in some sort of pain…for him.

But, hey, what was life without a little excitement and pain? Rock was definitely used to both. So he listened while Dusty explained what he had in mind and they planned on heading out first thing in the morning.

Gravel was still grumbling to his dad about how stupid "Injun Style" hunting was nearly an hour after they started out. And actually, he'd been griping since the night before when his dad had told him the plan. Gravel thought it was stupid, mostly because he'd have to get up when it was still dark, an idea that never sits well with any teenager.

"Just be glad I talked him outta the loin cloth idea," Rock muttered under his breath as he led his horse through the trees, following Dusty.

"It's danged cold to have your junk out hangin' all out in the open."

Rock felt like an idiot and completely out of his element riding bareback, especially since he was riding one of Dusty's most ill-tempered horses, an Appaloosa named "Demon Child." Rock thought he'd been aptly named. He'd already had to smack the horse on the rump a couple of times when he'd started acting up. It was a real challenge to hang onto the back of a grumpy, jumpy horse when you didn't even have the benefit of stirrups. But Dusty had insisted.

"We gotta do it like in the Old West," he'd argued the night before over Jack Daniels and RC. "We ride bareback, usin' bows."

It wasn't until Rock had three Jack and RCs—mostly Jack—that he'd agreed. Sounded like a great idea at the time. A way to prove themselves to be manly men. Of course, that was the alcohol talking and everyone knows alcohol never says anything wise.

But now, riding the skittish horse bareback in the freezing cold while fighting a pounding headache and upset stomach, the idea of it all just was sort of making him want to puke.

Gravel was still grumbling about missing breakfast, being cold and having his man junk squished on the horse's back. Rock silently seconded those complaints and added a few of his own.

"You don't got no 'man junk', boy," Dusty told Gravel. "You got tiny little baby junk," he teased.

"Do not!" Gravel sat up straighter to defend his manly parts and kicked his horse to get up alongside Dusty.

"I got man-sized parts, old man. Not like yours, that're all shriveled up from lack of use."

Dusty reined his horse in and turned to look at the boy. Probably out of lifetime of habit, he leaned down to lay his arm across the saddle horn, which, of course, was missing on the bareback horse. Rock chuckled when the old man almost fell off and had to grab the horse's mane to right himself. Dusty gave him a good glare too and then turned back to Gravel.

"I'll have you know that my junk is in great workin' order." He grinned and turned to hock another tobacco loogie suspiciously close to Rock's leg.

"Ask your gramma how good my junk was workin' this mornin'," he drawled with a lecherous wink.

"Ewwwww!" Gravel replied, his face contorted with complete and utter mortification at the thought of his grandmother having marital relations with her husband. Rock once again seconded that thought. The mental image…he shuddered the thought away, but the bile had already started rising pretty high in his throat. *In fact...*

Dusty laughed uproariously for a long time at the sight of his son-in-law losing his cookies over the side of the horse. Rock wondered how the old man was managing to hold his head up, much less laugh, since he'd drank nearly twice as much as he had the night before.

Once Rock was done losing his stomach contents—and Gravel, too, once his father started barfing and with the visual image of his gramma and Dusty still in his mind to help toss the cookies—they continued on toward the meadow Dusty insisted had the most deer.

"Now, when we get up there, you two shut your yaps and just hold still in the trees. The deer will show themselves soon 'nuff. Oh yeah, we're also gonna shoot 'em at full gallop."

Rock was still bristling at the "shut your yaps" comment, like this was their first hunt or something. Why, he'd been hunting and fishing since he was old enough to hold a rifle or a pole! How dare that old man say such a thing. If he weren't so old—and such a tough ol' bugger—Rock would've given him a sock in the mouth. No, he didn't want to hit the old guy—for one thing, Beglenda would kill him if he bruised her new husband—but he was pretty sure the old guy wouldn't waste any time hitting him back, and his head was already on the verge of exploding as it was.

But he was about to give the old man a piece of his mind when the "full gallop" comment worked its way into his hung-over brain.

"Full gallop?" he all but yelled, then cringed as the pounding increased in his head. He then had to whack Demon on the butt again when he tried rearing.

"Are you nuts? We're ridin' bareback, for Pete's sake! Just how do you think we're gonna ride at full gallop?"

Dusty looked at him like he was stupid. "You lean forward and grab the mane."

Rock rolled his eyes and winced at the pain that action caused. "And how do you 'spose we're gonna hang onto the reins and the mane *and* hold a bow?"

Dusty reined the horse again and rubbed his face as he thought. Then he grinned and looked back at his son- and grandson-in-law.

"We hold the reins in our teeth."

Rock and Gravel glanced at each other. They both knew from experience that such things were not going to end well. But manly pride wouldn't let them back down. Nope. They had reputations as bad ass—uh, bad dudes. No matter what, they were not going to weenie out.

They finally arrived at the edge of the meadow, and sure enough, after just fifteen minutes or so, the herd appeared. Surprisingly, there were two bucks in the herd—or maybe it was two combined herds—and Dusty motioned to the boys to get ready.

So, bows in hand, knees gripping the horses' sides and reins between the teeth, they spurred into a full gallop and bolted into the meadow. The herd all looked up and not a single deer moved a muscle. Rock supposed they were all probably trying to figure out what the heck they were seeing. Or maybe it was a second of silence before all the deer burst out laughing.

But in the time it takes for a grown man to realize that he has a really weak gag reflex and that holding reins in his teeth with a pounding headache and a stomach that was still threatening to toss what was left of its contents all over the horse was not a good idea, the deer sprung into action and bolted for the safety of the trees.

Dusty was leading the pack and managing to keep his seat while shooting a couple of arrows with complete grace. Rock narrowed his eyes, suddenly suspicious that the old man had done this before, that this wasn't his first eighteen hundreds style rodeo, or maybe he had some Native American in him and this stuff maybe just came naturally.

His father-in-law missed both of his shots (which squashed Rock's thoughts of his having done this before) and was fumbling behind him to get another arrow out of his quiver when Gravel saw his opportunity to show up both his dad and his step-grandfather, so he kicked his horse into warp speed and took off into the trees after the herd.

"Shhtttpphmm, dddrrzzuhhkkkllfff!" Dusty said through the reins. Rock raised an eyebrow at him and Dusty rolled his eyes, then pointed toward the trees.

"Shhtttpphmm, dddrrzzuhhkKKLLFFF!" He must have realized then that he could take the reins out of his mouth, because he spit them out and yelled, "Stop him, there's a cliff over there!"

Rock looked at him with a frown. "A cliff? This area is so flat you can see tomorrow coming!" He just knew the old fart was pulling his leg.

"No! There's a cliff just past these trees! I ain't kiddin'!"

Something in Dusty's tone told Rock that he was, in fact, not kidding and he then had that moment of parental terror when their child is about to put themselves in mortal danger—like when they run down the driveway toward a busy street, or dash out between parked cars in front of a truck barreling through a parking lot. Or when they're maniacally tearing through the woods on a bareback horse with reins in their mouth and trying to shoot deadly sharpened projectiles at three hundred pound animals who are running for their lives toward a cliff that they'll surely avoid, but said child likely won't.

And, of course, Rock was also terrified of what would happen to him when Skillet got her claws on him if he let her firstborn plummet to his death. But he knew that was selfish thinking, so he tried to push that aside and concentrated on getting to his boy.

"GRrrrvvurrr! Dddrrrzzuhhkkkllfff!" he yelled. But Gravel just completely ignored him and continued on his death ride.

"GRRRRVVURRR!" he yelled again, then realized he still had the reins in his mouth. He jerked them out and then yelled, "GRAVEL! STOP!"

But of course, the boy wouldn't listen. He probably thought his dad wanted to shoot the first deer. That was what he, Rock, would have thought if he'd been in the boy's boots. Rock yelled to stop, that there was a cliff; that he better listen or else he was gonna be in a world of hurt; if he didn't stop he was gonna lose his Xbox for a month; that he wasn't too big or too old for a butt blistering; and if he died, his Mama was gonna kill him…again.

Nothing was working, so Rock did the only thing he could think of to put an end to the kid's sure plunge and painful demise. He jammed the reins back into his mouth, then pulled an arrow from his quiver, notched the bow and took what aim he could while galloping at full speed. Then he let the arrow fly.

Some would have said that was a hard decision, the sacrifice. And in theory, maybe in a rhetorical discussion over a beer or three, Rock would agree. But in that moment he didn't even think about it. Didn't consider the ramifications. It was just a matter of choice: collecting his son's broken, bloody body from the bottom of a ravine, or picking him up off the forest floor? He could always later claim it was an accident, a stray arrow shot in the heat of the moment.

Gravel wasn't moving when Rock dismounted beside his body. His son was just lying there peacefully, flat on his back, looking like he was taking a nap in the woods. Rock kicked him lightly in the thigh with his boot. His head was *really* pounding now, after all that excitement, anger and fear.

Bending over was out of the question.

Gravel's eyes shot open and he frowned up at his dad. "What happened?" he asked with a dazed look.

"Shot your horse," Rock replied.

Gravel sat up then and winced as he rubbed the back of his head and looked around.

"You shot King? Why?"

"You were headin' toward a cliff, you moron. You wouldn't stop, wouldn't listen to me." Rock shrugged.

"I had to do somethin' to stop you. Figured gettin' you thrown off your horse was the only way."

King walked up to them at that moment and Rock could swear the horse glared at him.

"It was just a flesh wound. Quit bein' a baby," he muttered to the guy as he looked at his right rear flank where a two inch red gash was trickling blood. It was going to need stitches. Good thing Beglenda was back at the ranch house. She probably had some tendon of white wombat or some other crazy thing to use for stitching wounds in her witch's bag.

He rubbed the horse between the ears. "Just a scratch." King snorted and threw his head, as if to say, "You're a lyin' SOB. And you shot me. I ain't forgettin' that." Demon snorted too, then, as if in agreement.

Rock pulled Gravel to his feet just as Dusty arrived. His eyes took in the scene, and hocked a loogie at Rock's feet. The tobacco juice splashed on his boots and he scowled up at his father-in-law.

"Nice shootin', boy."

Rock nodded. "Thanks." He didn't bother telling the man he had been aiming for the horse's lower leg, but his hands had been shaking pretty badly at the time. If his aim had been any more off, he might have hit his son. He shuddered then, thinking about what all *that* would entail and started shaking all over.

"Welp," Dusty drawled, "we're gonna have to track that herd now. They ain't gonna come strollin' back into the meadow after bein' chased halfway across the county."

They ended up chasing the deer herd halfway across the county, but just a few hours before dusk, first Dusty shot a buck, and minutes later, Gravel got one. Rock didn't even try—he had decided his hands were never going to stop shaking and he didn't want to take a chance of hitting something—or someone—he wasn't aiming at.

So with Gravel and Dusty dragging their kill behind their horses, Rock took the lead. About three miles from the ranch house, a rabbit, or a squirrel, or maybe a tiny little beetle, ran across their path and Demon spooked. The cantankerous equine reared up on his back legs and with no saddle or stirrups to cling to, Rock rolled off his back like a sack of potatoes off the grocery store shelf.

But just throwing his passenger wasn't enough for Demon; oh no, he decided to "crow hop," which in horse terms means "stomp the jerk to death with our sharp, iron-clad hooves while putting all one thousand of my pounds behind my effort."

After making sure Rock didn't have any breath left in his lungs, and that he was a broken, bloody mess, Demon took off through the trees, whinnying with what Rock, in his dazed, concussed mind, thought sounded just like joyful laughter.

Dusty and Gravel appeared above him while he tried to suck just a whisper of breath back into his lungs. Dusty, true to his form, hocked a loogie before imparting his pearls of wisdom.

"You shoulda leaned forward and grabbed his mane."

Results: One trip back to town via Air Ambulance; one very large hospital bill due to a week-long stay for a cracked sternum, fourteen broken ribs, a broken jaw, a broken tibia and fibula (that's both bones in the lower leg for those not in the medical profession), and yes, another concussion.

Bowling For Brain Donors

The guys in the shop had a tendency to get bored easily (remember the Cheetah stories?). Like I said, Rock tried his best to make sure they always had something to do, even when business slowed down, but he wasn't always successful.

So when the floors had been swept, trash cans had been emptied, the bathroom (gag) had been cleaned (as well as young mechanics will clean a bathroom—which means basically just taking the spray washer and blasting every surface), the new tires were put on the racks and the nuts and bolts were in their proper places, the guys would go looking for trouble.

Today's trouble started when Kite (so called because he was always higher than a...) told the other guys about a show he'd seen called "Bowling for Bucks." One of them thought that sounded like a good game, and someone else said a deer should be involved (these guys were invariably thinking about killing some defenseless animal) and a round of ideas ensued over how one could "bowl for bucks," in a literal sense.

Well, as the worst ideas often do, this one came about by chance. Or bad timing. Maybe it was just karma. Something like that. As the guys were discussing what would work as a "bowling ball" that they could roll down a hill to knock a buck off its feet, the delivery driver showed up with a truckload of agricultural tires. You know, those big mo-fos that go on tractors, excavators, et cetera. The really big, heavy tires. The ones that are big enough for a human to fit inside. Sigh. We all know what's coming, don't we?

And so, off went the moe-ron squad, to the top of the hill behind the shop that led to the pond (yes, the same pond where the poor widdle deer lost its life to a flying oil filter the winter before). There were quite a few ducks on that shallow pond and the guys thought it would be great fun to use the them as bowling pins. Maybe they might even get dinner out of it, if they actually managed to hit one. Flattened duck a la orange. Of course, Jimmy had to point out that the game would then have to be called "Bowling for Bucks or Ducks."

It was decided Kite should be the first to travel by tire, since he was the one who had mentioned the bowling thing in the first place, and also because he was stoned enough to agree to it and to maybe not get injured. Too much, anyway.

Kite got into the tire as Gravel and Jimmy held it steady at the top of the hill. "Hey, there ain't nothin' to hang on to," Kite complained once he sat inside the giant rubber donut.

"You don't gotta hang on," Jimmy informed him with an authoritative voice, like he really knew what he was talking about. "The centrifugal force will keep you inside once you start rolling."

"Really?" Gravel asked with no small amount of awe in his voice.

Jimmy shrugged and muttered out of the side of his mouth, "I dunno. Sounded good though, right?" Gravel grinned and nodded.

Kite apparently wasn't too sure about that, or maybe he was just trying to process Jimmy's comment and trying to sort through a myriad of marijuana-coated memories from his high school science classes.

"Three, two, one, go!" Gravel yelled and let go of his side. Jimmy was still holding on to his and frowning at Gravel.

"What is it with you and counting down?" Jimmy asked before rolling his eyes and letting go.

And he was off! Kite's tire wobbled a bit from the lopsided weight, but it didn't take long for it to straighten out and gain speed. A lot of speed. So much speed, in fact, that when it hit the bottom of the hill where the pond bank was, instead of going onto the pond like the guys had planned, the thing launched right on over the pond in a leap that would have made Evel Knievel jealous. And in about two seconds flat, the pond was devoid of ducks…not because Kite had actually managed to *hit* any, but because they flew off the second they realized a giant rolling object was coming their way. Ducks apparently are much smarter than redneck mechanics.

And to be honest, the jump wasn't really that impressive, because it *was* a small pond, but still, the way that tire sailed over it was pretty cool. The guys thought so, anyway, as they whooped and hollered enough to draw Rock's attention from his nap—uh, office work.

Once again, Rock found himself trying to find the crew he paid good money to work. But they weren't working. He scowled as he stomped through the showroom floor, then into the shop, out the side where the dumpsters were (and where Kite and some of the others were fond of hiding when they were wanting to smoke weed), then he took a deep breath to get his temper under control (it didn't work) and to help lower his blood pressure (that didn't work either) and then he opened the back door to the parking lot, pretty much terrified at what he was going to find.

Yep, sure enough, there was his crew, screwing around in the back of the parking lot once again. He clenched his teeth at the sight of the idiots whooping and fist pumping the air. They were definitely up to no good, because "no good" always caused the most cheering with their group.

He wondered what the heck they were up to and stood in the doorway, pondering. They couldn't be hunting with the Cheetah again, though. For one thing, it was chained to the wall in the shop and locked with an industrial padlock. *But locks and chains can be cut…*

Rock shook his head. The guys wouldn't dare do that, not after he threatened to not only keep all their paychecks *and* fire them if he ever caught them messing around with the Cheetah again, unless he was there. He didn't bother to tell the guys he himself didn't want to miss out on any fun. He had to act responsible, after all.

But Rock wondered if he had been specific enough with the guys. They were the type you couldn't use more than two-syllable words with, after all. Did he actually tell them they couldn't ever *hunt* again during work hours, or did he just say they couldn't hunt with the Cheetah? *Dang it...*

He stormed over to where they were and it was then that he saw something that made him wonder if the top of one's head *could* actually explode, like an internal scalping. Or if steam could come out of your ears. It was a genuine concern, because at the moment it sure felt like something was going to have to give in the general vicinity of his head. The pressure was a'buildin'.

Because there, at the bottom of the hill, were twenty-six hundred dollars' worth of agriculture tires. In the pond. In the mud. One was even across the pond in the weeds.

It wouldn't have been so bad, and the tires could probably have been cleaned and put in the showroom and no one would be the wiser that they'd been unceremoniously rolled down a hill, but those tires were a special order for Ben Hamilton, one of the crankiest old men he'd ever come across. The man would make even his granddaddy look like a teddy bear. He was the definition of grouch.

Ben was calling the shop every day, sometimes twice a day, wondering if his tires had come in. This had been going on for two weeks. As of yesterday afternoon, he'd started threatening lawsuits if Rock didn't have them by today. Rock had assured the old fart that yes, his tires would absolutely, positively be in this afternoon. Since Ben had paid in advance, Rock really couldn't blame the man for being so cantankerous about his order. Plus, his excavator had been down waiting for the new tires, and that meant the man wasn't making any money. He was due to arrive at any moment.

"What in the (insert at least five four-letter curse words here, and maybe one six-letter one) are you (some more curse words. Just use your favorites. I'm trying to clean up my own mouth, personally, so that's why I'm not writing what Rock said. And honestly, it would be enough to make a group of longshoremen who used to be sailors who grew up in a construction site blush) doing?"

This time, it was only four eyeballs staring at him—belonging to Gravel and Jimmy. All the other nimrods were down in the field, in the pond, or beyond. Despite demanding an answer, it took just a second for Rock to figure out what they might be doing and since the two dummies just stood there flapping their yaps like a couple of big-mouthed bass gasping for air, he yelled down to the others.

"Get your (you know the drill) up here right now!"

Sure enough, eight more eyeballs stared up at him and Rock was beginning to feel like he was in a bass fishing competition with all the flapping mouths in the area. It took a minute for their brains to get enough oxygen to process his order, but finally they started climbing the hill. Rock rolled his eyes.

"Bring the (blankety blank) tires with you, you imbeciles!"

"But, boss," Bill whined, "the tires are too heavy to get back up the hill."

Rock was sure his back teeth had cracked from the force he had just exerted on them and again he thought about the various avenues the pressure in his blood could take to relieve itself from his body. It kind of felt like the pressure might be trying to escape from the back of his eyeballs. He wondered briefly just how far eyeballs could shoot with that kind of pressure behind them.

He turned to Jimmy and Gravel who had finally stopped gasping for air and ordered them to get the winch line.

"And bring the reel of rope too," he yelled back to them. "I don't know if the cable is long enough."

Sure enough, the winch cable wasn't long enough to reach the tires at the bottom of the hill, but after tying the rope to the winch hook, they were able to get all the tires back to the top of the hill.

"You know, boss," Jimmy said as they looked at the giant pile of tires now lying at the top of the hill, "Gravel and me didn't get a chance to try it out. And you neither. We got the winch now to pull them back up and all... maybe we could just try it out? Seems fun..."

Jimmy always knew how to get to him. Just sound really sad, like you were left out of something awesome, the only kid in the class who didn't get invited to the birthday party and all. Rock was, and is, a big softie at heart after all. (Just don't tell him I said that. He *does* have a rep to maintain.)

Forty-five minutes later, after Rock dizzily stumbled out of the tire after his third turn down the hill, he suddenly remembered that Ben was due to arrive at any minute and he reluctantly put a stop to what he'd aptly named "Bowling for Boneheads," since they'd made a game out of lining up at the bottom of the hill while one guy rolled down in a tire, trying to hit them. Needless to say, there were numerous bruises, tire marks and lots of vomit in and around the tires, and on the guys.

The guys were still cleaning the mud and debris and puke off the tires when Ben arrived. Rock groaned. If only the guy had waited just a half hour longer to get there, they might have gotten away with it. But, no, Jimmy had left the shop door open and Ben had a great view of the shop—and his pukey, muddy tires—from the showroom.

Results: Loss of thirteen hundred dollars, after being forced to give Ben a half-price discount, no matter how much Rock argued that the tires were just going to get muddy and possibly puke-filled after he put them on the excavator; a whole lot of bruises and a broken nose and a lot of whining.

Church Ladies And Shotguns Do Not Mix

Gramma Lizzie (remember her? Skillet's grandmother. Nice lady. A little crazy…it runs in the family) was a chicken lady. Hey, don't judge—there are cat ladies, right? Lizzie just happened to love chickens.

Said chickens were honestly spoiled rotten and out of control. The rooster, Stalker, was especially awful. He had three-inch spurs (okay fine, maybe one-inch) that he would use whenever the idea would enter his little pea-sized brain that he needed to shred something. Usually stray dogs and mailmen. But that rooster loved Gramma Lizzie and protected her like she was one of his hens.

Rock couldn't even walk in the yard without Stalker flying after him, screeching and pecking and occasionally flying up on his back so he could dig those spurs in. Rock really hated that rooster.

One day Rock and Gravel went over to Gramma's to help her hang plastic over her windows, because she'd complained that it was "getting cold." It was August, after all. Gramma Lizzie was always cold, by the way. She was the queen of layer dressing. The old woman was rarely without at least one housecoat and two pairs of socks, no matter the time of the year.

Rock laughed when he'd pulled into her driveway and Gramma Lizzie opened the side door to wave at them—she had on a dress with pants underneath, a long sweater over the dress, a shorter sweater over that, a knit cap on her head and a shawl around her shoulders. In August. Did I say it was August?

Gramma had an eight-foot chain link fence that ran around her yard, mostly for keeping chickens in and four- and two-leggeds out. Anyone who knew Lizzie knew to use the side door of her house and avoid the front yard, because…Stalker. That rooster had made it his personal mission to rid the county of solicitors and Jehovah's Witnesses.

There was a gate on the chain link fence with a latch on it that only a human should have been able to open, but apparently Stalker was able to use his spur as an opposable thumb, because the guys had barely gotten around to the side door when the stupid rooster came running around the front yard—outside of the fence—and jumped up on Gravel's back, and proceeded to claw the tar out of the kid.

Well now, Gramma Lizzie loved that rooster, but she loved her alien great-grandson even more and when she saw that darned ol' foul fowl attacking precious Gravel, with poor Gravel screaming and slapping helplessly at his neck where the rooster had grabbed hold of him and Rock chasing son and bird, trying to catch one or the other, it just set Gramma off. She went back inside.

And came out with a twelve gauge. By that time, Rock had managed to catch Gravel and get the stupid rooster off of his son.

"Put him back in the truck!" Gramma yelled as she leveled the twelve gauge at the now-strutting rooster who was so proud of himself for protecting the driveway from the evils of a five-year-old.

Rock complied and then BOOM! Feathers were flying. Rock looked at the now still rooster body lying on the driveway, quite impressed with the fact that the old lady had shot that bird's head off.

"We're having chicken for dinner," Gramma called over her shoulder as she went back in the house.

Stalker was soon replaced by a very nice rooster named John Wayne. John Wayne was much less temperamental and never attacked without provocation. I think one of the chickens must have filled him in on exactly what would happen if he did.

So I told that story to get to the next: One afternoon Gramma Lizzie called her grandson-in-law at his shop.

"I need help," she said as soon as he answered.

When an eighty-something-year-old lady says she needs help, you darned well better be ready to do whatever she needs you to do.

Rock was already up and grabbing his car keys, thinking about how many horrible things could possibly be happening to the poor, sweet woman, when she added, "The stinkin' foxes got into my yard last night and ran off with a chicken. They beat up John Wayne too."

Rock paused once he realized there wasn't any true emergency. A beat up rooster and a missing chicken weren't high on his list of things that would get him running.

"And what exactly do you need help with, Gramma? You're more than capable of blasting them into bits. I've seen you with a shotgun." Rock waved away the strange look he got from a customer at his comment.

Gramma Lizzie huffed. "I'm fine with shootin' in the daytime when I can see. It's the night I gotta problem with," she complained. "You know I don't have good night vision and that's when the foxes come out...at night. Right?" She said it like he was a moron and he almost laughed.

Rock moved back around the counter and sat back down. "Okay, so I'm guessin' you want me to come over tonight and help you shoot the foxes?"

"Yep, that's 'zactly what I want you to do. I'll even cook dinner for you. I know that granddaughter of mine don't cook you any nice meals—just that hamburger box stuff. Nasty." Rock could swear he heard her shudder—it was probably her old bones rattling. He had to agree with her though; that box stuff *was* nasty.

"How 'bout some chicken fried steak?"

Well, she didn't have to ask him twice. He'd do just about anything for chicken fried steak. And Gramma Lizzie was right—Skillet used to cook when they first got married, but she got lazy real quick and wouldn't cook, not unless it came from a box. Rock sure couldn't cook—he burned water. So any time someone offered a home-cooked meal, he was on that like a bum on a baloney sandwich.

When Rock got to Gramma's, he walked into the kitchen and the first thing he saw was John Wayne on the kitchen table. In a picnic basket. On top of a fluffy towel. And the poor rooster was wrapped in several layers of scarves. It was probably eighty-five degrees in the house. He didn't think chickens could sweat, but John Wayne looked like he'd just run a marathon. In July. In Phoenix.

"Is he okay?" Rock asked, indicating the poor rooster slow cooking in the basket.

Gramma looked over her shoulder where she stood at the stove. "He'll be fine," she replied. "He just needs some TLC for a few days."

Rock bit his tongue not to question her idea of "TLC." The poor bird looked like he was getting some "KFC" treatment instead—roasted chicken.

After dinner, Rock and Gramma went outside and put some chairs in the driveway, facing the front yard where the chicken coop was. The sat and talked about Jesus (Gramma's favorite topic) and cars (Rock's favorite), and about the family, friends and those who didn't fall into either category, until it got dark. And then they quieted and waited.

Sure enough, not long after the sun went down, the foxes came. Rock was going to wait until the little darlin's were forcing their way under the chainlink so he could see where they were getting in, but Gramma had other ideas. She grabbed her shotgun, jumped up and blasted a shot off in their direction.

"I thought you couldn't see in the dark!" Rock hissed at her as he ran toward the opposite side of the house where the foxes had run.

"I can't," she answered. "Well, not good enough to shoot the little monsters."

The two of them chased the foxes across the field behind Gramma's toward the cemetery, which didn't have a fence around it to mark the boundary. When they passed a headstone, though, Rock stopped in his tracks.

"Gramma," he hissed, "we're in the cemetery!" The idea of standing among all those dead people creeped him out a bit. Probably more than he wanted to admit.

"I know that," Gramma muttered back as she grabbed his arm to pull him along. "These people don't care that we're here."

"But we're walkin' all over the graves!" Rock protested.

He was pretty sure she had rolled her eyes in response, but it was hard to tell in the dark. An owl or…something…called out then and Rock was pretty sure it was one of the poor souls crying out in protest of being stepped on.

"Gramma!" he hissed again. "We can't be in here. We gotta go!"

"Not 'til we get those darned foxes. Look," she said, "over there, by that mausoleum thing…I'm countin' three, maybe four."

Rock had to squint to see where she was pointing and he gave the old woman a sidelong glance, now seriously doubting her claim that she couldn't see well in the dark. *He* could barely see and his eyes were fifty years younger.

But, sure enough, there were four foxes running in and out of a big gazebo looking thing. Rock shuddered, figuring there was probably a coffin in there, with a body inside…or bones. He started imagining a skeleton rising from a crypt and seeking his vengeance on those who dared to wake him from his eternal slumber.

*I seriously gotta quit watchin' them scary movies…*He shook himself from his thoughts, but couldn't help watching the trees, fully expecting someone—or some*thing*—to jump out at any moment.

Gramma Lizzie was creeping toward the foxes and Rock knew for sure that the old lady *could* see in the dark, because she had spotted those foxes just fine and was closing in on them like Elmer Fudd stalking Bugs. With an impatient wave, she motioned to him to hurry up.

Rock had to bite his tongue to keep from grumbling and saying what was on his mind—that she had tricked him into coming tonight. But hey, he got some chicken fried steak out of the deal. Can't really argue with that. And, he realized, he sure wouldn't have wanted Gramma out here in the haunted cemetery by herself (okay, maybe it wasn't really haunted, but it was still freaking him out).

Gramma motioned to him to go around the left side of the creepy mausoleum while she started circling around the right side. The foxes had run inside once again and Rock made a mental note that if one of those things came out with a bone in its mouth—any bone—he was outta there faster than he could say "Oh my God, I'm gonna die."

He crept down the side of the mausoleum, which was really big and Rock wondered just who was inside it, because their little county had never had anyone of note that he knew of, not anyone who rated such a fancy bone box. It was then that he heard a blast. A shotgun blast. Followed by a little ol' lady's cackling "woohoo!" Rock started runnin.

"Coming to you!" he yelled, so the crazy woman wouldn't shoot in his direction. When he got around to her side, she was already chasing another fox across the graves. Rock rolled his eyes. She definitely didn't need his help at all—she ran faster than a World Cup soccer player and obviously could see about as well as a puma in the dark.

BOOM! BOOM! She shot twice more and Rock sighed in relief, knowing she was then out of ammo.

"There's one more I left just for you, son!" she yelled.

"Seriously?" he muttered under his breath. She'd managed to actually kill three foxes, in the dark, while running. Three shots, three kills...the woman really should have joined the Army and been a sharp shooter.

"Night blind my a—"

"Hurry, Rock! He's gonna get away!" Gramma's shriek interrupted his mutterings.

Rock was stumbling more than running at that point, since his eyesight apparently wasn't as good as hers. He saw movement to his left and aimed his shotgun, but he wasn't really sure what he was seeing, so he hesitated to shoot. It would just be his luck to blow Mrs. Johansson's cat to bits. It was likely—the woman lived on the other side of the cemetery and she had a cat house. Like, literally…the woman owned dozens of the furry cactus creatures. The county's crazy cat lady. She was in good company with Gramma as a neighbor.

Gramma once again yelled at him to take the shot and so he assumed she was talking about the object moving up ahead. He squinted, trying to make out the shape…but really, a cat and a fox look pretty similar. Deciding Mrs. Johansson probably wouldn't miss one cat if that's what it was, he took the shot.

Apparently, Gramma's sharpshooting abilities didn't trickle down the genetic line to in-laws, because he didn't hit whatever the creature was, but he did manage to blow a headstone in half. *Dang it…*

Gramma was disgruntled with him and letting him know exactly how she felt, without actually saying any curse words. She was a good Baptist, by golly—she'd wash her own mouth out with a bar of Dial soap if she said anything harsher than "darn."

"Gimme that gun, son!" she exclaimed as she tried to jerk the shotgun out of his hands. Rock didn't want to be shown up by an eighty-something old lady and argued with her over the gun for a minute, until she relented and let him take another shot.

BOOM! Dang it, he missed again, but at least he didn't hit a headstone this time. Nope. Hit a tree and took off so much bark that he contemplated a new method for felling trees in the future.

It was right at that moment that Deputy Robbie showed up, lights and sirens alerting the entire county to his presence.

"What in the (blankety blank blank blank—at this point, Gramma threatened to wash Robbie's mouth out with Dial) do you two think you're doing?"

"We're shootin' the foxes that are killin' my chickens," Gramma told the officer, like that was all he needed to know about the reason they were blowing up the cemetery.

Robbie sputtered for a minute before he could think of an answer to that. "You can't just shoot rifles in here!" he yelled. "You coulda killed someone!" He swept his arm to indicate the neighbors who lived near the burial grounds.

Gramma scowled at the deputy and crossed her arms over her chest. Rock noted absently that her boobs were *under* her arms.

"First of all, young man, we weren't shootin' rifles. These are twelve-gauges. Secondly—" she swept her arm around the graves, "who are we gonna kill? They're all dead already!"

Robbie's face got so red then that Rock could actually tell that it *was* red —and he was colorblind and it was dark as sin out. *This ain't good...*

The deputy actually got himself under control and didn't blow up at the old lady. Rock was impressed at his self-control. He himself was ready to choke her.

Results: Rock was charged with "Reckless Endangerment" and "Discharging of a Firearm in a Residential Neighborhood." Both charges could have been felonies, but thankfully, the judge had a good sense of humor—and was the local Avon lady—so after agreeing to several hundred hours of community service and purchasing several hundred dollars' worth of Avon, Rock was off the hook. Gramma didn't get charged with anything, because...Gramma.

Chapter 5 ANIMALS ARE WEIRD

This section of this chapter of this book is a conglomm…conglamer…comglomer…a collection of goofy things that happened to Rock over the years involving animals. Because, after all, this chapter is about animals, right?

Shifty Sheep

I'm sure I already mentioned that Rock had a small ranch. Well, yeah, I did mention that, because a lot of the stories so far have revolved around that ranch (or Dusty's large ranch, in case you got confused. I stay confused, so it stands to reason that I might go around spreading my pearls of dumb-dumb everywhere I go).

On this small ranch, Rock had a variety of animals: a small herd of cows, a handful of horses, a dozen sheep, a couple of goats, various fowl and of course dogs and cats.

Most of the time the animals behaved themselves in animaly ways and didn't move beyond the scope of what is expected of the four-legged (or two-winged) species. Every once in awhile, though, the craziness of the humans apparently infected the animals and they'd do something…unexpected.

Like the time Rock went out onto the back porch to enjoy his morning coffee in the fresh mountain air, his favorite summer routine. As he sipped the coffee just the way he liked it—hot, black and bitter, like his soul (and Skillet said she liked her coffee like her men—ground up in an airtight bag in the freezer)—he looked around his ranch, a feeling of satisfaction seeping through his bones at the beauty he was blessed to possess. Colorado was truly God's handiwork.

The cup was still at his lips when he noticed something strange—the sheep were all lined up along the pasture fence, just a few dozen yards away. That was a bit strange, but not really *that* unusual. Sheep were herd animals, after all, so if one decided he was going to stand at the fence, then it sort of stood to reason that the others would follow. But the fact that they were lined up in a perfect row with nearly equal spacing between each sheep was really creepy.

However, what got the hair standing up on the back of Rock's neck was the fact that the sheep were all staring at him. Just looking at the porch with their gold-colored, unblinking eyes. Like they knew something he didn't…or like they were waiting for something.

He frowned, unsure why they were staring at him like that; it wasn't like the weirdos were hungry and waiting for him to feed them—they were standing in a pasture of soft, green field grass, for Pete's sake. And he had given them scoops of sweet feed in the barn the night before. Same as always.

But what made Rock decide he should head back to the kitchen to drink his coffee was the fact that when he moved to the porch rail to get a closer look, all twelve heads turned in the direction he moved. In unison.

Apparently they were Stepford Sheep.

Stinky Kitties

One of the major on-going problems at the ranch was an infestation of unwanted animals. No, I'm not talking about the Stepford Sheep. What I'm referring to are things like pine tree gobbling porcupines, garbage can destroying raccoons, and the lovely black and white kitties with the ultra-concentrated sack of stench parked on their behinds.

Rock was going to feed the cows one winter morning and Pebbles, who was just a tiny little speck at that time and barely walking and talking, wanted to go with Daddy. Being the good sort of daddy, Rock obliged the little darling.

It was bitter cold that morning and Pebbles was all bundled up in her one-piece snowsuit and staying in the warm truck while Daddy did his chores. Rock was loading hay bales into the back of the truck when he heard the little darling's voice say excitedly, "Kitty!"

Rock turned around to see which cat had wandered down to the hay barn, but it wasn't any of the cats they employed as mousers. No, this was a very large black kitty with a white stripe down his back that was inching its way toward Pebbles—who had managed to open the truck door and climb out—with his tail straight in the air.

He had just a second to act. Not only are skunks obviously stinky to the max, but they also are know to be rabies carriers. It would be bad enough if she went home smelling like something that had died, been buried for a few weeks, then dug up and left out in the sun, only to then be doused with vinegar and wrapped dirty gym socks—but if he took her back home to Skillet, aka Mama, foaming at the mouth and trying to bite everyone, well there would be hell to pay.

Acting quicker than he probably ever had before, Rock leapt toward his daughter and grabbed her by the back of the snowsuit and launched her into the truck. He then grabbed his shotgun from the gun rack behind the seat, because the stupid skunk had decided to attack him. It was charging and hissing and doing this funny little dance that Rock figured was supposed to be a threat, or maybe the skunk was just mad because Rock had removed a new plaything from him. Either way, when the skunk actually bit the toe of his boot, Rock decided the thing must have rabies, because he wasn't even trying to spray. So he shot it.

When he got back in the truck, Pebbles was sniffling, and Rock knew that waterworks were coming. He thought he might have hurt her when he flung her into the cab, but she wouldn't answer him when he asked. Of course, her vocabulary at that time was limited to approximately fifty words (a situation that would very soon—and very painfully—be remedied when she started non-stop conversing).

Rock had exhausted his dad-knowledge of what could be wrong, so he asked if she wanted some hot chocolate and when she nodded, he drove her back to the house.

Once Pebbles was out of the cumbersome snowsuit and sipping her hot chocolate while Skillet put frozen waffles in the toaster, Rock went to his gun safe to get some more shells for the shotgun. When he walked back into the kitchen, he was met by Skillet brandishing one of those egg turner things.

"Why is *my daughter* crying?" (The kids were only "hers" whenever it was a convenient excuse to get mad at her husband.)

Rock shrugged. "Dunno. Thought maybe you could get her to tell you."

She turned to Pebbles and asked the same question he'd asked her before. Pebbles started crying harder.

"Daddy killed da kitty!" she wailed.

Skillet, who really loved her dogs (but not Rock's) and most of the cats, spun on him with a raised eyebrow and a swinging egg turner thingy.

He immediately defended himself with hands raised. "A skunk! Skunk! I shot a skunk!" he yelled as he spun around to head back out to finish his chores, but not before he heard another wail..

"Daddy killed da kitty!" Pebbles again bawled as he left. She'd never get over that one. Her daddy was a kitty killer.

Demo Bears

It was still dark one cold spring morning when Rock headed out to the barn to get some sweet feed for the sheep and goats. He was halfway there when he heard a strange noise that sounded like a bulldozer plowing through the bins he kept the feed in and he ran the rest of the way. When he got in the barn, it *looked* like a bulldozer truck was trying to crawl into the bins. A big, black, furry bulldozer.

A rather large black bear was face down in the biggest bin, butt up in the air and back legs kicking, helping himself to the fricking expensive specialty horse feed Rock had to buy for one of his mares that had problems pissing. He had just stocked up on the stuff the day before and had even bought steel feed bins, just for this reason. Apparently the bins weren't bear-proof. Having just spent over five hundred bucks on feed, seeing that big ol' black furry butt in the air while it's owner helped himself to the grub kind of ticked Rock off.

So without thinking (obviously), Rock grabbed the nearest large object he could find, which happened to be a two by four lying by the door. He stomped right up behind the bear and whacked him as hard as he could across his furry black cheeks with that board.

Now the "without thinking" part comes into play here. Did you know that a black bear can run faster mad than a human can scared? Did you also know that when a scared human leaps into the nearest vehicle, a mad black bear can break truck windows? He can also rip off door handles, side mirrors and even decorative molding. In fact, a *really angry* black bear that, oh, say just got smacked across the hiney with a rather large piece of wood, can slash tires and even rip a bumper completely off.

A really, really, *really* angry black bear can basically turn a thirty-thousand-dollar truck into a tin can of crap in about five minutes.

Satan the Crotch Killer
And then there was Satan.

Not the *real* Satan, the Prince of Darkness, Beelzebub, Lucifer, et cetera, but Satan, as in the stray cat who showed up at the ranch and announced, with inch long bared fangs and a hiss that would have made Dracula cringe, that he was the new barn cat.

Satan was aptly named. The cat was pure evil. Ugliest thing you ever saw, too. He had only half an ear on one side and the other looked like it had been ripped right down the middle. He was missing fur in several places and his tail looked like it had been stripped by a half-blind toddler using a pair of square scissors. He had a scar running through one of his eyes and down his cheek (said eye was clouded over and obviously blind). And to top it all off, he had one fang longer than the other, so he always looked snaggle-toothed.

This hideous cat was a terror. Just like his namesake, he sought to kill, steal and destroy. His entire purpose and joy in life seemed to revolve around turning every human in his presence into nervous wrecks.

"Oh, come now," you say, "how can an innocent little kitty make anyone nervous?" Well let's see: Satan liked to hide up on the barn rafters and wait until someone walked underneath before swooping down like some crazed flying squirrel, landing on that poor person with all his nails spread out like talons on a bird of prey. Then the cat from hell would hide under cabinets, rolling tool carts, et cetera, and whenever any unsuspecting soul would get close enough, he'd swipe at them with the aforementioned razor-sharp talons. If you were working under a car (which the guys in the auto shop would, of course, do quite often, duh), the cat would stalk you like a cheetah after a gazelle on the plains of the Serengeti, stealthily inching ever closer until he was close enough to rip your leg, arm, man bits, et cetera, to shreds.

Whenever Satan could entice one of the female barn cats to get close enough, he'd leap on her too, pinning her down with nails and fangs, then proceed to noisily and painfully knock the poor girl up (sorry, animal activists, these are barn cats—as in strays, and you can't exactly take them into the vet to spay/neuter). When the poor cat would have her litter—usually in the small den the cats had made under a cabinet in the workshop—Satan would turn into Super Satan.

Super Satan was capable of feats of great strength: faster than a speeding beer can; more powerful than a gas-powered hedge trimmer; able to leap tall mechanics in a single bound. Any foe (aka, anyone working in the shop) who dared to near his den of ill-repute would suffer his wrath. Most often in the form of shredded skin.

One day little Pebbles, in about her third year, came toddling into the shop to see what daddy was doing. The guys were all working hard to get some roll cages made for their race cars for the coming weekend and weren't paying much attention to the little girl.

Pebbles sat on the concrete floor, happily sorting nuts and bolts into coffee cans when she saw some movement out of the corner of her inquisitive little eye. It was a baby kitty! Her very most favoritest animal in the whole wide world! They were soft and fuzzy and she loved the way their tummies rumbled when they purred. Getting to hold a kitty was better than anything in the whole wide world.

Pebbles just had to see the little darling up close and personal, so she innocently put her life—well, at least her soft, unmarked skin—in danger and crawled over to Satan's den of ill-repute. Bet you know what's going to happen, huh?

Nope, you're wrong. Apparently, Satan didn't think Pebbles was any kind of threat at all, because he didn't so much as hiss at her as she gently pulled kitten after kitten out from under the cabinet and put them in her lap so she could love them and squeeze them and call them George.

It wasn't until Rock needed a fresh battery for his drill that he noticed his daughter was sitting on the floor with the devil's progeny curled up on her lap, all six of them. She was lovingly stroking the soft fur and every few minutes or so, she would pick one up and kiss it on the head.

It was such a sweet sight, it would make anyone smile and say "ahhhhhh." But considering who the father of those little fur balls was, all Rock could do was scream "AHHHHHHHHHH!" which of course caused Pebbles to jump, which made the kittens all fall off her lap and start mewing, which caused mama cat to dart out from under the cabinet (where she was probably getting some much needed sleep thanks to her unexpected babysitter) and grab the babies one by one, running back under the cabinet to safety. The sudden lack of kittens made Pebbles wail like she'd just lost her best friend—which, in her three-year-old mind, she had.

It was then that Satan jumped down from his post on the rafter above. He sauntered over to the crying Pebbles and gave her a precursory sniff. Rock tensed, ready to kick that cat clear through the barn wall if he so much as twitched a claw at his daughter, but the danged thing actually rubbed her arm. Like he was trying to comfort her. Rock couldn't believe his eyes.

But then the Evil One turned toward him and Rock could swear the cat actually narrowed his freaky yellow eyes at him.

The cat actually started stalking him. Like with his back fur up, hunched down on his haunches, talons extended long enough to make a Samurai double-think his sword length, stalking. Big ol' Rock, who was as tough as stewed skunk and would charge hell with a bucket of ice water, was feeling seriously intimidated by the thing. So much so that he backed away from the hissing, stalking monster and kept backing until he fell backwards over Jimmy, who was hanging out of a car, welding.

When Rock was flat on his back, seeing stars from hitting his head on the hard concrete, he had three thoughts: One, thankfully the furry demon hadn't so much as spit near Pebbles; two, the stupid cat was now leaping through the air towards him, talons extended, aiming right for his crotch.

And three: it was a good thing he was done having children.

Super Coon

You know those playful little striped bandits everyone thinks are so cute? Yeah, raccoons...not playful. Destructive. Capable of shredding paper, plastic *and* metal. A pack of them could decimate a trailer park in nothing flat. Like mini coonados.

One of the little darlings was wreaking it's coonie havoc in Rock's barn. It was getting to the point that things—expensive things—were getting destroyed. After an entire sack of sweet feed had been ripped open and scattered all over the place and then a seventy-two bale hay stack had tumbled over after one of the little pirate animals had decided to make a nest at the bottom, which in turn knocked over a hundred-gallon water trough that in turn soaked the stalls (which of course had needed mucking) turning the manure into a disgusting poo soup, Rock had had enough. He grabbed his rifle and headed out to the barn.

Did you know that raccoons are really fast and agile? And that they can leap from barn rafter to barn rafter with the ease of a trapeze artist while being shot at? Rock emptied his rifle trying to hit the darned thing and had only managed to shoot his barn roof full of holes.

Rock is actually a darned good shot, but shooting at something supernaturally (okay, maybe not *supernaturally*) quick and slippery like that is nearly impossible, even for the most expert sharpshooter. So in a blind fury (he might have been feeling just a teeny tiny bit like a fool at that moment, or at least like a bad shot), he stomped off to his house to get the double-barrel twelve-gauge shotgun.

Even a horrible shot can hit just about anything with a shotgun. A blind old lady with Parkinson's and one arm tied behind her back can probably hit a target with a shotgun. The darned things blast a giant hole and you pretty much just have to point the weapon in the general direction of your target and pull the trigger.

Because of the possibility of supernatural abilities in this particular raccoon, Rock actually missed hitting it with his first shot. Instead of hitting the wily thing, he blew a twelve-inch diameter hole in his barn roof. Rock growled and clenched his teeth at the sight of pre-dawn stars shining though the roof—it was yet another thing he would have to fix. He reloaded and looked up at the ceiling.

Rocky (yeah, Rocky Raccoon…not very original, but, eh, I can't always be clever) hopped from one rafter to the next and Rock was pretty sure the stupid thing was laughing at him. He took careful aim and planted his feet. This time, the jerk was getting both barrels.

BOOM! This time, the sound from the double barrels going off reverberated off the barn walls and Rock was sure everyone in the county had heard it. He *had* to have hit the darned thing that time.

And he had—when the bandit had leapt across the rafters once again, Rock could see that the very tip of his tail was now hairless. The rafter where he'd been sitting at the time of the shot was missing a rather large chunk of wood. The splinters were still falling to the ground.

Rock scowled. The shot hadn't even drawn blood. Cursing in words that would make that sailor slash longshoreman slash construction worker guy blush, Rock broke his barrel and dropped some more shells in. Just as he closed the barrel and took aim again, he heard a loud CRACK.

It wasn't just a creak, like when an old building settles, or even the creaking crack sound a roof makes when there's more than a foot of snow on it. No, this was more like the sound of a heavy wooden beam cracking in half, just before it comes crashing down on top of the customer's custom classic Jaguar you had parked in your barn and covered with a ridiculously expensive car cover to keep it out of the weather and away from any dust or dirt while you waited for a part to ship from England.

Rock stood there in disbelief. Shock. Dread. Fear. Thoughts of leaving the country filled his mind just then. Not that Rock would necessarily be afraid of the average irate customer, but this particular car owner just so happened to be the brother of a mobster. Yep, an old-fashioned mobster, like as in Italian mob, just like those portrayed in "The Godfather." The nail your knees to the floor or put a horse head in your bed kind.

He was envisioning all the horrible things that could happen to him, the goodfellas who were going to show up to fit him for cement shoes before tossing him into his own pond. Or maybe they'd just drag him behind their Lincoln Continental down the two-lane country road for a few dozen miles. If they were merciful, they'd just put a bullet in the back of his head.

And to top it all off, the raccoon was sitting on the next beam over, laughing at him. Rock was sure of it this time. His mouth was curled up in what sure looked like a grin and a funny noise was coming from his little black lips that sounded suspiciously like *hahahahaha! Sucker!*

Bugger That Badger

Driving two-lane country roads can be dangerous, to both human and animal alike. The area where Rock lived had a road that wound through the woods and you were always in danger of plowing into a deer, a skunk, or (if you were lucky) a raccoon.

One day Rock was riding with his friend, Brian, in a two-door Honda CRX, one of those really low to the ground itty bitty baby cars that are so popular with teen girls. Now Rock and Brian are both really big guys and they had no business whatsoever trying to shove their oversized frames into a car the size of a tennis shoe, but there they were, shoulder to shoulder, with a combined weight of a juvenile elephant, and the Barbie car was nearly bouncing off the ground. In fact, Rock could swear he was feeling rocks hitting his butt.

They had just come around a curve when something equally low to the ground and furry ran out in front of them. It was too late for Brian to stop, so he just gripped the wheel extra hard and hit the poor little thing. Sometimes these things just couldn't be avoided. Literally.

Neither one of the guys was prepared for exactly how hard that hit was going to be. It was like the car had hit a speed bump. Or a boulder. Or maybe another small car.

After the impact, Brian stopped on the shoulder, well off the side. The unwritten rule of the country back road is that you remove the road kill when you hit it, so the next person didn't hit it too. So, the big guys unfolded themselves out of the tin can to retrieve the carcass. Rock pulled his gloves out of his back pocket in preparation of picking up a bloody animal that probably—and most likely—had guts hanging out. Gross.

When they came around the back of the car, they could see a tannish furry thing in the middle of the lane. Brian walked toward it with Rock following close behind.

"What is it?" Rock asked. It wasn't very big, but from the way it threw the car into the air, it should have been a several hundred pound creature.

"Dunno," Brian said as he cautiously toed the poor little thing. Rock moved around him and reached down to grab the back leg, ready to fling it into the woods.

The "poor little thing" chose that moment to miraculously come back to life. It wasn't a gentle resurrection either—nope, it was a hissing, clawing, scratching, biting revival. Rock immediately let go and he and Brian both yelled, "BADGER!" as they ran back toward the car.

Badgers, for those who don't know, are notoriously mean and vicious, and really tough. They aren't just defensive creatures, like maybe a porcupine is when it throws its quills to protect itself. No, a badger is offensive too… and vindictive. They will stalk you if you have wronged it in anyway and seek revenge. They're like the little Italian mobsters of the animal world.

The two linebacker sized guys flew back into the car (probably taking a bit of door frame with them as they did) and slammed the doors. Thankfully, the badger seemed to be satisfied with their retreat, as he meandered back into the woods.

After about ten minutes of sitting in the car awaiting the Return Of The Badger (that would make a good horror movie title), the guys cautiously got back out and surveyed the area. No badger could be seen. There wasn't even any blood on the road. Brian and Rock looked at each other with shared confusion.

"I know danged well we hit it," Brian said.

"Yeah," Rock agreed. "No doubting that, with the way the car launched." He shrugged. "Oh well, let's get back."

They forced their bodies back into the car much more slowly this time and Brian turned the key. The motor made a strange sound and Rock said something about checking it out when they got back.

It was probably a half mile down the road before the guys realized what was wrong with the car.

Steam started pouring out of the hood. "Broken radiator, or loose hose," Rock guessed.

And then the temperature shot up, which was expected with a radiator issue. Brian pulled over and they cautiously popped the hood. Steam shot up and the motor was hissing and popping. Rock checked the hose, which was intact, the looked underneath. Sure enough, there was a big crack in the radiator. And then he noticed the oil spill under the car.

"Uh, dude, looks like you're gonna have several hundred in repairs," he told his friend, "and that's if I do the work for free. That danged badger cracked your radiator and took out the oil pan. We're gonna have to get a tow."

And the silly creature just walked off into the woods, not a scratch on him. I said they were tough…

Owl Be Darned

Rock was heading down the same country road (maybe I should have named this section "Country Roads, Kill Me Now") with another friend who shall remain unnamed (Rock seriously can't remember who it was…age can do that to a person). They'd headed in to town to grab some burgers and fries for the guys in the shop and were on their way back.

As was typical of a lot of vehicles in Colorado, Rock's truck didn't have air conditioning, because he never needed it that high up in the Rockies. Until this year, that is. This particular year, Colorado was hotter than the Sahara desert in July, for some reason.

So the guys were cruising down the road with the windows down and bullsh—uh, b.s.ing as guys will do, just talking about nothing and everything, when this whirlwind of fluff flew in through the passenger window and proceeded to whip around Rock and his friend.

They were under attack, only they had no idea from what; it was moving too fast. But whatever it was, it had claws and sharp wings. They batted at it and covered their faces and probably screamed like little girls (not that they're going to admit that). Rock apparently forgot he was supposed to be driving at that moment, because they went flying off into a field (thankfully, they were past the woods at this point) and he nearly flipped his truck before he got it stopped.

Once the truck was stopped, the object of attack decided it was safe to land, because there, sitting calmly on the dash just above the radio, sat a little barn owl. An itty bitty barn owl, probably a juvenile, for the record. He sat there, just turning its head back and forth, blinking at them. He was a cute little thing, although he looked a little bit angry and a whole lot crazy. But that was to be expected—the poor little guy had probably never had a ride in a Dodge with two rednecks before.

After a few moments, the owl seemed to be calming down, so Rock reached over to gently pick him up so he could release him out of the window. The owl apparently had other ideas, because the little fluff ball flew up before Rock could even touch him and proceeded to frantically fly around the cab again, beating the men and shredding them with his talons.

Rock and the unnamed friend were screaming like little girls again, trying to cover their heads and faces while swatting at the bird. They both were desperately trying to find the door handles to escape, but since they couldn't see what they were doing, they were sort of trapped. Finally, Rock got his door opened and stumbled out, while Mr. NoName crawled out of the passenger window, falling into the prairie grass and scampering away from the truck.

The two men approached each other at the front of the truck while keeping a wary eye on the little bird. He had calmed down once again and was perched on the top of the steering wheel, blinking at them through the windshield. He had an angry expression on his face and screeched, a sound that Rock could swear said, "It's my truck now, bee-atch," but he didn't speak fluent owl, so he couldn't be sure.

"Now what?" NoName asked.

Rock shrugged. "Open to suggestions."

The guys stared at the owl for a few minutes. "Maybe if we wait long enough, he'll get bored or hungry and fly away," NoName suggested.

As if he heard and understood, the owl turned his head and looked down at the seat, where the fast food bags sat. Rock and NoName looked at each other.

"Surely not..." Rock said, but surely yes, the owl hopped down on the seat and out of sight. Out of sheer curiosity, the guys cautiously moved around to the driver's window to see what he was doing, and sure enough, the little bird had opened one of the bags and was working on getting a burger unwrapped.

"Shoo shoo!" Rock said to the bird, who just turned his head and glared at them. Rock put his hands up and silently watched as the tiny owl got the burger unwrapped and then nearly swallowed the hamburger patty whole, discarding the bun and toppings on the seat. Rock was thankful that he'd been cheap and opted for vinyl seats.

"Dang, that stupid bird is going to eat all those burgers," NoName said as they watched the bird grab yet another burger out of the bag.

"Not much we can do about it, not unless you want to try tackling him again," Rock replied as the owl tossed some French fries down his craw.

"Heck no," NoName said while shaking his head violently, "that thing's crazy. I ain't touching it." Rock was in full agreement. The thing might be little, but he was as vicious as a flying badger.

The two guys just stood there and cringed each time the bird pulled out a burger from the bag. When it was all said and done, the tiny bird that couldn't have weighed more than five pounds had eaten six hamburger patties and nearly a full order of large fries, before he finally flew out of the cab and off, back toward the woods.

Rock could swear he heard a "burp" as he flew away.

Goat Tokes

Then there was the day when nothing was going right. You know those days—you stub your toe getting out of bed; put your shirt on backwards; stumble out to the kitchen limping on your boo-boo toe, only to realize you didn't set the timer on the coffeepot the night before; the truck's battery is dead because you left the dome light on; et cetera. You know how it is. A Murphy's Law day.

This was one of those days for Rock. All the above had happened to start the day out on the worst possible foot (yeah, with a broken toe) and it was only getting worse. Like when Robbie, the county deputy sheriff, showed up to question him about a report of some stolen cars Rock had purchased from his brother-in-law.

Rock denied the cars were stolen; his brother-in-law (Skillet's baby brother), Shifty (yeah, I know, dumb name, but hey, it fits), had given him the titles to those cars, for Pete's sake. Robbie then informed Rock that the Motor Vehicle Department had reported a break-in a few weeks back when a stack of blank titles had been stolen. Rock could feel his world crashing down around him at that point. He should have know better than to make a business deal with someone named Shifty.

While Rock was standing on his back porch talking to Robbie (and ignoring the Stepford Sheep, who were once again lined up at the fence and staring at him with a "you're an idiot, you know?" expression on their little faces), Rock noticed that, just behind Robbie, next to the barbeque grill, a very large and lush marijuana plant was growing.

Beglenda (yes, the mother of Shifty and Skillet), had a weed addiction. Like, smoking a quarter pound a day addiction. And whenever she was at their house, she would smoke on the porch. Apparently, she cleaned out her pipe, seeds and all, by the barbeque grill.

Also apparently, marijuana seeds cultivate very well in greasy soil, since the weed was growing where the overfull barbeque drip pan, well, dripped. So for those of you who want to grow your own Mary Jane, you might want to try hamburger for fertilizer. Just sayin'. (Disclaimer: The author in no way promotes the cultivation and/or use of illegal narcotic substances. Check your state and federal laws for the legalities of such. Wow, that sounded pretty good, huh? All legal-like. I have goosebumps.)

Now this was back in the days before Colorado had legalized the stuff. So when Rock noticed the plant growing just a few feet away from a law enforcement officer, and said plant was large enough to dump felony charges on his head, Rock's eyes must have had a look of horror, terror, or just plain freak-out, because Robbie started to turn around to see what was causing such a look. Rock immediately asked if he was going to jail to keep the man from turning, and Robbie must have thought that fear caused it, because he thankfully redirected his attention at his grand theft auto suspect.

Robbie scratched his chin and thought about it. Rock knew Robbie was well aware of all of Shifty's shady deals (sounds like a used car dealership) and the man's long arrest record, so he figured the deputy was just drawing it out to make him sweat. He hoped.

"Well, now," Robbie drawled, "I'm gonna have to ask Sheriff Rogers 'bout that. Not sure if this falls under GTA too, but receivin' stolen property is a crime, ya know."

Rock really wanted to say "duh" to the annoying deputy, but he kept his thoughts to himself. Sarcasm probably wouldn't help the situation, especially not when dealing with a man who watched *Mayberry* reruns to get deputy pointers from Barney Fife. No sense of humor at all.

Rock couldn't help himself when he darted his eyes to the plant once again, like it was going to grow another foot while they stood there, or maybe start doing a dance like those fake plants that danced to music. Robbie started to turn around again to see what had caught his attention.

"So," Rock drawled to bring Robbie's focus back to him as he moved to the other side of the porch and leaned down to pick up a hose that had been left carelessly out for someone—probably him, with the way the day had been going—to trip on, "do you really think Shifty broke into the MVD?" he asked as he started to coil the hose.

"I mean, that's a felony," he continued. "He ain't never done nothin' more than petty crimes before." It was then that he realized the hose was moving in his hand and he looked down, realizing in horrified shock that he had mistakenly picked up a bull snake.

Since Rock is no fan of snakes, he may or may not have screamed like a sixth grade girl before launching the poor thing clear across the yard toward the sheep pen. Robbie laughed so loud that Rock was worried he might split his sizable gut and had to rethink his earlier assessment of the deputy. Apparently, he *did* have a sense of humor.

Robbie looked over to where Rock had tossed the unsuspecting snake and it was then he noticed the Stepford sheep lineup. He stopped laughing then and frowned, then glanced at Rock, then back at the sheep. Rock could tell he wanted to ask a question, like "What the hay-ell is wrong with those sheep?" but Rock acted like there wasn't anything strange at all going on, like it was normal for a herd of sheep to stand at attention in a regimented line so Robbie was probably afraid to look stupid. Rock was just glad the man's attention was riveted on the little weirdos.

But, of course, true to the way his day had been going so far, a breeze kicked up at that moment and Rock cringed. He knew from the many times he'd been over to his mother-in-law's that marijuana plants had a really strong smell. He was pretty surprised that Robbie hadn't at least smelled the darned thing by now and made a mental not to strangle his mother-in-law when he saw her next. Or maybe he should.

Robbie finally asked the question. "What's the deal with them sheep? Kinda weird how they're just starin' at us like that, ain't it? And standin' all in a row..."

Rock didn't answer and just shrugged. He had no answer. He'd mentioned the ovine chorus line at dinner one night when Beglenda had been over. Skillet had said he was crazy or drunk, but Beglenda had decided that the sheep had probably been abducted by aliens, who had either replaced them with alien sheep robots, or else the aliens had implanted brain-control devices in the animals and they were now recording the humans' every movement. The woman really did smoke too much weed.

Which reminded him of the plant. He cleared his throat to draw Robbie's attention. All he needed was for the guy to look just a little to his right and down...

Robbie shook his head and turned back to Rock, all business again. He started listing all the things he would have to do to—get the VINs off the cars; take possession of the titles Rock had gotten from Shifty; blah blah blah, when Rock noticed that William, Pebbles' pet billy goat, was sauntering toward them from across the yard. The darned thing was always getting out of his pen and causing problems. Rock wondered briefly if the guys had put the freshly painted Impala back in the paint shop, or if it was still outside in wandering goat territory. That would not be good.

William had managed to work his way up to the pot plant while Robbie was listing all the things that would need to happen before he would decide if Rock would be arrested, or not. Rock was barely listening, since the plant was more of a concern at the moment.

He watched as the goat took an experimental nibble off the plant. His slanted eyes nearly bugged out of his head once he tasted it, and he soon devoured the whole thing. Rock wondered if that much weed could be toxic and then wondered how much money he could get for THC laced goat meat. Thinking of the hippie throwbacks who lived in Boulder, Rock thought, *I might be on to something here...*

By the time Robbie was done reciting his list, William had managed to eat all the leaves and flowers off the pot plant and was stumbling around the yard, eyes half closed and drooling. When the stoner knocked over a trash barrel, Robbie turned at the noise. Rock didn't try to distract him this time. The goat had managed to eat all the evidence.

"What's wrong with that goat?" Robbie asked, a frown on his brow as the goat stumbled and then bumped off a fence post before sitting down on his haunches like a dog. William then ducked his head and started scratching the dirt with his horns. Robbie looked back at the sheep chorus line and shrugged.

"You got the weirdest animals in the county," he muttered as he ambled off toward his car.

Elvis The Alky

The stoned goat brings to mind Elvis, the alcoholic pig.

Rock had a friend who had gotten a cute little piglet because he was told they make great pets. They do, if you starve them half to death to keep them small. But when they grow to two hundred plus pounds with the strength of a small hippo, then sometimes they're not the best pets after all. Being really smart and stubborn, they will figure out just how to get their way, and sometimes that means throwing their weight around. Literally.

Rock offered to take Elvis off his friend's hands, since he had a ranch and the pig would do just fine there. At first Elvis was a little intimidated by the other animals, but once he realized the other animals were all just a bit on the weird, alien-abducted side, he figured he would fit right in and proceeded to declare himself Boss Hog (hahahaha, see what I did there? "Boss Hog"… snort).

Elvis loved to wander into the work shop when the guys were working. He carried around a sixteen-inch Chevy dually hub cap that doubled as his food bowl and would toss it in the general direction of whoever was closest, a not too-subtle-hint that said "I'm hungry, feed me now."

The guys didn't mind Elvis; in fact, they thought he was pretty funny with his grunting and bullying and pushy ways. Guess he reminded them of their wives.

One day after a particularly grueling day working on some race cars, one of the guys broke out a case of Bud Light. He set the box down on the floor of the garage and the guys all moved chairs, tires, boxes, et cetera, around in a circle and proceeded to relax in the time-honored tradition of men—drinking and b.s.ing.

Elvis came into the shop about then and looked at the testosterone circle. Deciding *he* needed to be in the circle, he pushed Jimmy off his stack of tires and shoved his way into the middle next to the case of beer.

"If you wanted a beer, you just had to ask," Bill quipped as he pulled a bottle out and set it on the floor next to Elvis.

Now pigs are pretty curious and they have a really good sense of smell. Elvis apparently liked the smell of beer, because he took the bottle in his mouth and chewed a bit on the top. The guys laughed uproariously at the sight of a pig with a beer bottle in his mouth, but Rock worried Elvis might break the bottle and cut himself. Just before he could take the bottle away from the pig, Elvis managed to get the lid off. He then set the bottle back on the floor, spit the cap out, then picked the bottle back up with his mouth, and tipped it back. Told you they were smart.

There was a moment of awed silence before the guys all broke out in cheers and excitement. And then a flurry of beer bottles being grabbed to see if Elvis would repeat the process.

Sure enough, the pig opened one beer after another, repeating his method over and over until there weren't any more beers. Of course, that led to a few guys running to town (well, they actually drove, since it was over twenty miles and running would take too long and shake up the beer on the way back).

Elvis was showing a bit of the effects of his beer consumption then, and Rock took pity on the guy and gave him some dog food (his favorite food... Elvis's, I mean) in his hub cap. The pig then lay down next to the empty beer box and took a nap.

Rock and the others found some busy work while they waited for the others to get back from town and it was then that someone noticed a strange noise. It sounded like a chainsaw with a loose chain, but moving on a low speed. No one could figure it out, until Jimmy realized it was coming from Elvis. He was snoring.

When the guys got back, they had bought another case of Bud Light and two cases of some generic cheap beer. Apparently, they didn't think Elvis deserved the good stuff. They obviously weren't animal lovers.

But the joke was on them when they woke Elvis up and they opened the box of cheap beer, only to find out that the case was cans, not bottles. They gave a can to Elvis, but he couldn't open the tab. So the guys ended up drinking El Cheapo beer while the pig got the good stuff.

Elvis got through another four beers before he again passed out for a nap in the middle of the shop. Rock took pity on him once again and covered him with a blanket and made the guys leave the shop so he could sleep. Rock is an animal lover, obviously. Bears, skunks and raccoons being the exception.

Well, word spread about Elvis the Beer Drinking Pig and when Rock and Skillet had a big barbeque party for the Fourth of July, almost everyone brought beer for the pig. It was a great thrill to give Elvis a bottle, watch him remove the lid (he had gotten really good at popping the lid right off by that time) and then chug the beer. Before long, Elvis was rip-roaring drunk.

Did you know that when a two hundred plus pound pig passes out across your driveway so that your guests can't leave, you can't roll, drag or in any other way remove said pig? An unconscious pig full of beer apparently manages to double his weight. Probably has something to do with barley and hops. Anyway, the guys had to get a furniture dolly and a winch and pull the pig up onto the dolly.

This was the beginning of Elvis's slide into the sad realm of alcoholism. He craved beer, so much so that he became obnoxious if you were drinking one and not sharing. And by "obnoxious," I mean that he would shove your chair over or bite your leg. Whenever Skillet would have a party—which was often, being that she liked to show off her culinary skills (just not with her family, who were subjected to hamburger meals in a box, remember?), Rock would have to lock Elvis in the barn to keep him from accosting any beer-drinking guests.

One night, Elvis took exception to his barn banishment, and he head-butted the barn door until the wood splintered and the latch broke. Out he came, a rampaging, alcohol-deprived, very angry pig on the run toward the guests.

There were screams of terror and shouts of confusion when Elvis came charging into the foray, slamming into guests and uprooting chairs. It looked like a scene from a B-horror movie, or maybe a show like "Hogs Gone Wild" (see what I did there? *Hog wild*...oh man, I'm cracking myself up). Rock shouted to be heard above the melee.

"Just give the pig a beer and don't make any sudden movements!"

It was shortly after that that Skillet insisted Elvis be banished to the cow pasture during parties, or else the well-marinated pig was going become ham sandwiches. Bacon. Pork loin.

Rock argued with her over that. "I'd be afraid to put his meat in the smoker...we'd probably blow up the entire ranch just from the fumes."

(Don't worry—Elvis lived to be pretty old for a pig before he died of liver cirrhosis.)

Chapter 6 YOU CAN'T PICK YOUR RELATIONS

Bearly There

Beglenda was crazy. Seriously crazy. Certifiably. But Rock loved her. She was adventurous. She was wild and, did I already say crazy? She was also stoned out of her gourd most of the time.

The woman would find the most insane things to do—rock climbing in order to search for petroglyphs, rappelling into deep ravines to look for treasure, sliding down into an old mine shaft to explore an abandoned silver mine.

Of course, *she* never did these things—she'd sit at the entrance/top/opening of whatever place she'd found and smoke a bowl while Rock got the honors of risking life and limb.

But Rock didn't mind. He was having fun, exploring, searching for mostly non-existent treasure. He was also getting away from the drudgeries of life, work, et cetera. And away from Skillet most of the time.

Once in awhile Skillet would actually accompany them on their adventures. She wasn't one to climb, crawl or even walk, really, but she would sit in the camp and watch the fire and the kids.

One time Beglenda had discovered a map that hinted some Spanish gold that had been stolen by a Native American tribe might be hidden in a cave. She was just sure she knew exactly what area that cave was located. She was positive she alone had solved the three-hundred-year-old missing gold mystery and that they were going to be rich. Rich, I tell you. (Insert somewhat maniacal cackling here.)

True to form, Beglenda waited at the entrance of the dark cave and filled a bowl (of her marijuana pipe, for those of you who are not schooled in the art of weed smoking…good for you, by the way. Just say no and all that), and proceeded to light it up while she yelled instructions to Rock as he went further and further into the deep, dark cave.

"There should be a turn not too far past that rock column," she yelled. "It'll be on the right."

"On the right?" Rock yelled back. "There's a column, but the tunnel is on the left."

Beglenda squinted at her map and then brushed off a hot ash that fell on the old paper. "Oh, sorry," she yelled back. "I had the map upside down.

Yeah, turn left."

Rock rolled his eyes and started muttering, something about how old ladies and weed shouldn't go together and why was he the only one who was going into the dark cave, when it would be Beglenda who would take the credit for anything they found. And besides that, Skillet would run off with any money they might get, he was sure of that.

He went a little farther and shined his flashlight around the walls of the tunnel. There was another cavern up ahead, but there was also another tunnel.

"Which way? Cavern or tunnel?" he yelled back.

"Mmm ummhbbenn," was her answer.

"What?" he yelled back. "I can't hear you!"

"Mmm mmuumhhmmm!" Was the answer.

"Arggg," Rock grumbled. Either Beglenda was too busy with her pipe, or else he was too far away to hear. Probably a combination. He had to make the executive decision.

Since the narrow tunnel would require crawling, he mumbled, "Cavern it is," and marched ahead.

As he ducked into the entrance, he shined the light up to the ceiling to see if he had room to stand. It was a pretty big cave, with maybe a ten foot ceiling. He moved the light around, hoping to see a wagon with trunks filled with gold coins. Something easy. It would be nice to find something with wheels, but with his luck, there would be one hundred thousand coins, each embedded in a slab of concrete or something.

He swept the floor of the cave with the light when he saw a large, dark lump in the corner. It looked like maybe it could be a chest with a tarp over it. Or hopefully, that wagon. Rock practically ran over to see what it was.

"Bear!" His yell echoed through the caverns as he ran for the entrance. "Bear!" he yelled several more times as he ran for his life toward daylight. He didn't want to risk his mother-in-law's life, but he sure wasn't going to stay in the cave and be a bear appetizer.

Rock flew out of the cave opening and grabbed his stoned mother-in-law's arm, dragging her with him as he went.

"Run downhill!" she yelled. "Everybody says bears can't run downhill!"

That sounded really stupid to Rock, but considering he could smell bear breath—and feel its heat on his neck—he decided it was worth a try and headed toward the ridge of the small cliff that they had climbed up just an hour before.

Guess what? The fact that bears can't run downhill is a bona fide falsehood. A big ol' fat stinkin' lie. Not only *can* they run downhill, they run even *faster* downhill. Like gravity takes over and makes them go into warp speed.

Rock and Beglenda were slipping and sliding more than they were running, but Rock was hoping they would be able to make it to the RV where they'd left Skillet and the kids. He started yelling warnings to his family to get into the RV. Even though he couldn't even yet see the campsite, he hoped they could hear. As much as he and Skillet didn't get along, he really didn't want to see her become a bear appetizer either…or more like an entrée, in her case. There would be questions, forms to fill out and all. He really wasn't in the mood to deal with authority figures.

Thankfully, Skillet apparently did hear his warning shouts, because she and the kids were inside the RV and watching through the window as Rock and Beglenda broke through the trees and ran across the clearing. The door was on the opposite side and Rock dragged Beglenda as they slid around the RV to the door.

Locked! The blankety-blank bleep bleep bleepity bleep woman had *locked the stinkin' door!* Rock banged on it and yelled all kinds of pleads and threats for a few seconds, but he knew he and Beglenda were out of time—the bear was coming into the clearing at that very moment.

"The ladder!" Rock yelled as he yanked his mother-in-law toward the ladder at the back of the RV that led to the roof. Being the chivalrous man that he is, Rock even let her climb up first, but he was hot on her heels.

"Fasterfasterfaster," he chanted as he pushed on her butt.

"I'm goin' as fast as I can," she complained back to him. "This ain't easy, you know!"

The bear had found them by then and was growling in complaint at his snack getting away. Rock knew he/she/it was just seconds away from standing up on those back legs and then he would be a goner. Bear bait. Rock salad. Man-atizer.

Beglenda launched herself onto the roof just then and Rock quickly followed, grabbing his mother-in-law and as he did, rolling the two of them away from the ladder. The bear did stand up on its back legs then, rising to its full height of eight feet. Rock could see the top of its ears and prayed that bears didn't know how to use ladders.

"Do you think he can climb a ladder?" Beglenda gasped, apparently reading his mind.

Rock himself was panting from their terror-filled trek. "I dunno," he wheezed. "What do the morons say who said they can't run downhill?"

Beglenda punched him in the arm.

Thankfully, this particular bear couldn't—or wouldn't—climb a ladder and soon got bored and wandered off back the way it had come. Rock and Beglenda waited another ten minutes or so to make sure the thing wasn't hiding behind a tree waiting to ambush them, and then climbed down. It was at that moment that Skillet came out of the RV. She was eating a sandwich, acting like nothing was out of the ordinary. *"My husband and mom being chased by a monster of a black bear? No biggie. Gee, I'm hungry..."*

Obviously, she didn't give a sh—uh, she didn't care squat about them. He shouldn't have been surprised, not really. Skillet had been planning her mother's funeral for years, even though Mom was only in her fifties. She seemed to be counting the days until she could get her family's small—really, really small—fortune. She seemed to forget most of that "fortune" had been spent over the years on bail money for Shifty.

Skillet also seemed bent on trying to get him dead, or so it seemed to Rock. He thought back to all the times she'd start a bar fight, making sure Rock was going to be forced to defend her in some way...and it was usually involving Rock versus two or three other guys. Big guys. Like biker body-builder crowbar-bending guys. Not that Rock wasn't a big guy himself and he could definitely hold his own in a fight, but when you pit two or three of the same makeup against another, the fight is a bit lopsided.

And then there were all those could-be-disastrous "accidents" Rock was the victim of and that Gravel was always behind. He'd asked the kid once if his mother had put him up to trying to murder him and Gravel had just laughed. *And lately my coffee has been tasting funny and now I'm getting stomach aches.* He made a mental note to check the stock of rat poison when he got home.

He frowned at the woman he'd married. "What the—I can't *believe* you—you just locked yourself in the RV, left us out here *with a bear*, and you make yourself a sandwich?"

Skillet shrugged. "Wasn't sure if bears could open doors," she replied around a mouthful, "so I wasn't taking any chances. And I got hungry." And with that, she went back inside and got a bag of chips.

Rattlers, Spiders and Bears…Oh My

Then there was the weekend when Rock and Beglenda—thankfully Skillet-less this time—went to Painted Canyon to see some cave drawings that were supposedly there and which may or may not have been drawn in order to give further clues about the stolen Spanish gold (yeah, we're still looking for it at this point).

The cliffs had some really cool petroglyphs, but you had to rappel down to see them. Getting to the cave was a little trickier—there was a path (Rock discovered that after risking his neck rappelling over the side), but it was hidden, very narrow and steep.

After seeing the petroglyphs and spotting the path, Rock climbed back up to retrieve the stoner and they were soon sliding down the path. That path was really treacherous and Rock was afraid Beglenda was going to fall right off into the ravine below, although the woman was high enough at that moment that she might just float.

And if the path itself wasn't bad enough, there was also a rattlesnake wanting to give them a two-fang tattoo every two feet. Seriously.

By the time they'd reached the cave, Rock was thinking he needed to smoke a bowl himself. His nerves were so frayed and his blood pressure so high, he figured explosion was imminent. He wondered again for the bazillionth time if eyeballs would shoot out of one's skull.

Being the chivalrous sort, Rock led the way into the cave. He wasn't really worried about a bear this time, because no bear in his right mind would made a cliff-side cave his home, but who knew what else they might find.

"What else they might find" turned out to be the world's largest spider web. Rock's skin crawled at the sight of it, afraid to find out exactly what the heck could have woven such a monstrosity. Thoughts of the gargantuan spider on *Gilligan's Island* filled his head. He figured the creature that made that web had to be at least the size of a Volkswagen Beetle.

That was an exaggeration, duh, fueled by Rock's overactive imagination, and maybe a little contact high too, since Beglenda had packed yet another bowl and was currently smoking it in the tight cave quarters. He was feeling a little dizzy, but less pressurized at least.

Around a rock column, they found the spider who made the web. He wasn't German car sized, but the danged thing *was* the size of Rock's hand, which is about the size of a grizzly bear paw, and was menacing enough to send the two humans hightailing it out of the cave. Rock swore he heard the dang thing hiss at them.

Not to be deterred after all they'd done to get down to the cave, Rock and Beglenda stood at the entrance and threw rocks at the spider. Rock managed to hit it with a good sized stone, but it didn't even bobble on its web, so he picked up a fist-sized rock and threw it as hard as he could.

The splat on the wall was pretty impressive, and the two speculated about others who might come upon the cave in the future, seeing the splat and wondering what the cave dwellers were trying to recreate with such a masterpiece. It sort of looked like a half-eaten piece of baloney.

Nothing else too exciting happened in that cave, but for those interested, there is a primitive drawing on the wall of a large masted ship. Sort of like what you might see if you saw a Spanish galleon. On a tribal cave wall. In the middle of Colorado.

Good luck finding it…and take a snake whacking stick and a large can of Raid.

Bat Sh*t Crazy

Beglenda found an old map of silver mines (don't ask…to this day, no one knows where she found this stuff) and wanted to go exploring. She was always looking to find that secret buried treasure; the stolen Spanish gold; the deepest, darkest, bear- and spider-infested hole for Rock to descend into.

It was this day that she'd found the absolute deepest, darkest hole for her son-in-law to. It was an abandoned mine shaft. No cave to walk into this time. Oh no. This time, a hole barely wider than Rock's shoulders awaited him.

Beglenda sat on the edge of the hole while he lowered himself down and smoked a bowl. She called encouragements down to him after every toke.

"Not too much farther, I'm thinking." Inhale, hold it, hold it, blowwwwwwwww.

"Probably almost there." Inhale, hold, blow.

"You hit bottom yet?" Tap tap tap (this would be Beglenda cleaning out her bowl. Rock could just picture a handful of pot plants growing at the mine entrance come spring).

For the first time since forcing himself into the tiny shaft, it had widened at that point and Rock suck in enough breath to answer.

"I'm close," he yelled back and was about to add that, actually, he couldn't see how close he was since it was too dark and he couldn't bend his head in the tight space to let his headlamp shine on the bottom, but before he could get another word out, a deluge of bats started flying up the shaft and right at Rock.

The bats were of course trying to use their usual method of exit from the mine after being startled, but their passageway was rudely blocked by a two hundred plus pound human. Rock found himself at the center of a batnado.

Flying rats were everywhere—battering his face with their leathery wings, slamming into his feet, his legs, his butt…and his man parts. He yelled and twisted around on his rope as much as he could in the tight space, trying to fight off the bat blitzkrieg.

"What's goin' on?" Beglenda called down, but Rock couldn't speak for a minute. He was afraid he might ingest one of the darned things. He held one hand over his face and swung at the creatures flapping around his head. *I need a bat bat, stat!* he thought, chuckling at his own cleverness. *Then they'll be flat bats...bat splat...* He pulled one out of his hair then. *Oh look, a bat hat.*

He finally managed to get stupid things off his head and they took off up toward the exit. He figured then he didn't need to explain what the problem was, since Beglenda's shrieks told him she'd encountered them by now.

After a few moments, she was back, peering down the shaft. "Ugh, I *hate* bats! You coulda warned me!?"

Rock grunted and rolled his eyes. "Well if I hadn't had four of the danged things trying to crawl in my mouth at the time, I mighta said somethin'."

"You okay?" Beglenda asked and Rock felt a little soothed. At least *she* cared if he was okay or not. Of course, he was her only source for a potential score of silver fortune…

"Yeah," he yelled back, "if you ignore the fact that I just got a flying rat enema. I might have to take a bat shat." He laughed at his joke as he lowered himself the final few feet to the bottom of the mine.

"You at the bottom yet?"

"Yeah, just touched down." The smell at the bottom of the shaft was nauseating, he assumed from the bazillion bats that were living down there.

"Do you see anything?"

Rock sighed. "I just touched the…uh, ground…a second ago. Gimme a minute!"

The "ground" was soft and squishy and seemed to be where the source of the stench was coming from. Rock figured he was probably standing in about a hundred year's worth of bat guano. That's poop, for all y'all who aren't in the know in regards to animal excrement. *It's a bat scat mat,* he snickered to himself. *I can do this all day...*

Beglenda asked again what he saw and Rock sighed once more. The woman was incorrigible and extremely impatient. He moved his head around so his headlamp could shine around the area.

"Just a bunch of bat shi—wait! There's something shiny on the wall!" This is what they were hoping for, that the silver vein might still be there in that mine, just waiting to be harvested. It was possible there was still silver in that mine, since they couldn't find the regular entrance to the place, and it was common knowledge that miners would often hide an active mine entrance to keep out thieves. Beglenda had speculated that maybe the miners had blown the entrance before some catastrophe happened, the mine owner died, et cetera, and no one had come back to finish mining.

Rock moved over to the area where he'd seen the shiny flash. He tried to ignore the way his boots were squishing in the giant pile of poo and the toxic stench cloud that wafted up with every step as he drew closer to the wall. Sure enough, on the mine wall was an area that had a metallic sheen. There was some dirty substance covering most of it—Rock assumed it was bat pee —and he used his sleeve to wipe it off.

"Is it silver?" Beglenda's excited call echoed through the cave.

"Nah," Rock called back. "It's a sign that says 'exit'."

There was a pause, then, "Seriously?" Her voice was so incredulous that he scowled.

"Yeah, seriously," he yelled. "What? You think I'm gonna lie to you so that I can come back here and dig silver outta the mine by myself?"

"Well, it is a possibility," she called back. Rock rolled his eyes once again and moved further into the mine.

It was pretty primitive as far as silver mines went. The walls looked like they'd been chiseled out by hand, and there were very few beam supports in the tunnels. It really did look like it had been the work of one or two people and not an organized mine company. Beglenda's theory that the mine had been abandoned by a handful of miners and then hidden until they could come back at a later date that never happened was starting to look possible.

Rock went into several small caverns and didn't see anything of note, but then he moved into a larger area, the largest so far. He had to step up into it, but he could actually stand up to his full height in there and he assumed it might have been the original cavern in the mine, and probably was where the original entrance was. But before he could figure out just where that entrance might have been, his headlamp apparently startled the actual colony of bats living in the mine.

The deluge of bats he'd encountered before had obviously just been stragglers, the standing-room-only crowd, because the group that was in the larger cave outnumbered them about a hundred to one. Maybe a thousand to one. All Rock knew was that bats were coming at him from every direction and all he could do was cover his head and hit the ground.

The "ground" in this cave was even more thickly covered in guano. He should have been clued in to that fact when he'd had to step *up* into the cave. There was likely a dozen or more feet of bat crap in there. And he was lying on it.

If that weren't bad enough, the sound from all those bats frantically flapping was nearly deafening and apparently startled, panicking bats urinate when they fly, because Rock soon found himself soaking wet.

It seemed like ten minutes before the flapping died down and that's when he heard Beglenda's screams and cursing. Rock knew the bats had found their way out of the cave via the shaft and he thought it might be safe to haul himself off the poo bed and make his way back out.

Climbing the rope up the shaft was a lot harder than it should have been, but his hands were covered in slimy poop and pee. As were his clothes. His boots. His face. And his hair. He was one big blob of wet bat crap.

It wouldn't have been so bad, but because he reeked so much, Beglenda made him ride in the back of the truck all the way home—over two hundred miles. In November. In Colorado.

Now he was covered in frozen bat crap.

Rocky Mountain High

The mother-in-law wanted to explore an area that, yes, she'd found on some obscure map. Rock wondered if she had a special supplier for obscure maps of never-before-discovered treasures, some guy in a back alley that "psssst'd" at people as they walked by. "Hey, lady, ya wanna buy a treasure map? Gotta special this week on King Solomon's Mine…two for one on Mayan maps…"

The area Beglenda wanted to explore this time was in an uninhabited area of the mountains, not accessible by vehicles, not even in Rock's jacked-up four wheel drive truck. So they drove as close as they could and then hiked.

It was a beautiful day in late winter—the sun was shining and it was warm. Spring was right around the corner and the birds were singing in the trees that were starting to bud. Rock was enjoying the day immensely, happy to get away from the craziness he called life. Nothing could ruin this day. (SPOILER ALERT: This day would, in fact, be ruined. Stay tuned.)

They could hear water running ahead of them and Beglenda asked to stop for a minute to "check the map," which meant she wanted to load another bowl. Rock could never get over the fact that the woman smoked cigarettes and weed like a coal train, but never seemed to get winded when they'd hike. He himself was huffing and puffing from the high-altitude exercise.

She lit the pipe and studied the map as she took a toke. "There's a creek up ahead," she said while holding her breath.

"Looks like it's got a bridge over it though," she finished as she let the smoke out.

Rock was pretty sure a bird in the tree above her just crossed his eyes and fell backwards off his branch, but he didn't say anything. *Talk about Rocky Mountain high*...his mother-in-law was going to be responsible for destroying an entire eco system when a whole slew of animals got the munchies and ate four times their share.

When Beglenda was done with her bowl, they marched on toward the creek. When they broke through the trees, Rock almost laughed. The "creek" was more like a raging river, one any seasoned white water rafting guide would be hesitant to travel down.

The water was overflowing its banks and rushing by in a flurry of white caps, which stood to reason, since it was apparently fed by snow runoff and they'd had a very wet winter. Logs and debris flew by them and Rock saw a beaver clinging to one of those logs with his eyes bulging out of his head, a "help me" look on his face. This wasn't good.

There *was* a bridge, just as the sketchy map showed. What the map neglected to show, however, was the fact that it was a rope bridge, and one that looked like it had been built from hand-woven prairie grass about two hundred years ago. And termites had been using it as an all-you-can-eat buffet.

They stood there contemplating the bridge that was swinging about three stories above that raging river. It wasn't something Rock wanted to even think about crossing. There was no way it was safe. No freakin' way. Beglenda sighed and Rock almost shouted in relief when he realized his mother-in-law had at last come to her senses. He started to turn back toward the trail, but Beglenda patted him on the back.

"You go first," she announced.

"Seriously?" he all but yelled as he turned to her. "Are you crazy, woman? Look at that thing!" He pointed to the bridge with both hands.

"It looks like it'll fall apart if a bird so much as takes a piss on it!"

Beglenda frowned at him and stepped a little closer to the bridge and seemed to examine it.

"Oh, now, don't be a drama queen. It isn't *that* bad. I'm sure people use it all the time."

"What people?" Rock exclaimed as he spread his arms and turned in a circle. "There ain't no one around here for twenty miles!"

Her frown turned into a scowl. "Well, someone had to build it, so it stands to reason that someone uses it!"

He snorted and rolled his eyes. "Yeah, someone built it *centuries* ago! It was probably Lewis and Clark!"

Rock was really exasperated with her at this point. She never seemed to have a lick of common sense when it came to dangerous situations—at least, not when *he* was the one being put into the dangerous situations.

Beglenda squared her shoulders and turned to walk back the way they came. "Well, if you're gonna be a chicken about it..." she muttered as she started picking up her things.

Rock gritted his teeth. He knew she knew that calling him a coward was the one thing that would get him to prove her wrong. He hated being so predictable...especially when it came to putting his neck on the line. *Don't say it...don't give in...she's manipulating you...don't...*

"Fine," he growled, mentally kicking himself for doing exactly what he told himself *not* to do.

"I'll go first." He pulled straps off his shoulders.

"At least hold my backpack. I don't wanna get my stuff wet if I go in." He pulled his wallet and cell out of his pants and dropped them into the outside pocket of his pack and handed it to the now grinning woman.

Getting his stuff wet was really the last thing Rock should have been worrying about at that moment. If, by some pretty likely chance that he *did* "go in"—into the raging river—staying above water without sucking in half the river would be quite a trick in itself.

The bridge creaked at first contact, when he'd barely put one foot on it. He glared back at his mother-in-law, pretty sure she was trying to get him killed. *Like daughter, like mother...*

"Did Skillet take out a life insurance policy on me or something?" he muttered and scowled further when she cackled.

"Not that I know of, but that's a heck of an idea." That was about the response he'd expect from her. He glanced back and saw that she was grinning. Rock looked heavenward and prayed for patience. And a safe crossing. And a new mother-in-law.

The boards were spaced about eighteen inches apart, which really wasn't that far—if you were walking down a road. But when you're trying to balance on a narrow, swinging, broken-down, old-as-time rope bridge, while taking careful steps onto boards that may or may not hold your two-hundred-fifty-pound butt, well, eighteen inches might as well have been five feet.

He'd managed to inch his way about twenty feet when the stupid thing started swaying. *Really* swaying. Like, "hang on for dear life, oh dear Lord, I'm gonna die!" swaying.

The sight of the water rushing by below combined with the swaying landscape was making him severely nauseous and if he weren't afraid of falling in, he would have leaned over the side to toss his cookies. Rock turned then to go back the way he came.

Beglenda was at the edge of the bridge, feet braced against one side, leaning back with both hands hanging onto the rope rail and...rocking.

"Hey!" Rock yelled at her. "What the (here's that four-letter word opportunity once again) do you think you're doing?"

She looked like the cat with the canary hanging out of its mouth as she smiled sheepishly and stepped back off the bridge.

"Just having a little fun," his mother-in-law yelled back over the noise of the rushing water. She waved dismissively at him.

"You're such a party pooper."

"Oh, go smoke a bowl," Rock yelled back as he turned his attention once again to the bridge.

"That also is a heck of an idea," Beglenda replied and she proceeded to do just that, leaving him to risk his life on his own without her "help."

Rock took a few more cautious steps out onto the still-swaying bridge and planted his feet far apart for balance. He felt like a toddler with a full diaper walking like that, but other than an elk or an occasional bear, who was going to see him?

"Hey, turn around and smile!" Beglenda shouted. He glanced over his shoulder and scowled. *Of course* the woman would have brought her video camera. *Great, just what I need—evidence.* Rock gave her a one-fingered wave and turned his attention back to the bridge.

There were quite a few boards missing, which meant rather large holes in places. Trying to step over the holes while maintaining his balance and not making the bridge sway any more than it already was swaying was quite a challenge and required his concentration. Beglenda was yelling something behind him, but he didn't really care what she was blathering about. She probably just wanted him to smile and wave at the camera again. He had half a mind to moon her, and if he didn't need both hands to hang onto the bridge, he'd do just that.

Rock was almost to the halfway point when he realized the bridge was starting to sag. Seriously sag. Like, we're talking a ten foot drop. Rock suddenly had visions of Indiana Jones in the middle of the ancient rope bridge, and exactly what happened when he cut one of the rope rails. Except, in Rock's case, there wasn't a huge gulf below him like Indy faced, which was good. But what *was* below him was a raging death river of freezing cold snow runoff. Which was not good.

The bridge creaked again and dropped another five or so feet. Rock wasn't moving by this point; it was all he could do to hang on while the bridge dipped and rocked. Beglenda was once again yelling something, but Rock wasn't sure he could turn around and see what her problem was. Any movement at that point could send him toppling into a sure fate as an ice cube. He could hear the eulogies that would likely be made at his funeral:

"Frankly, he was always a little cold." That would be Skillet.

"When they fished his frozen body out of that river, it brought a new meaning to 'on the rocks'. Get it? Rock...rocks...ice..." That would come from Jimmy—he wasn't the best at telling jokes.

"I still think with some cinnamon and cayenne oils, we can bring him back. Might need to add the blood of a Gila Monster..." Yeah, Beglenda.

"Can we eat yet?" That would be Gravel.

The bridge was vibrating then and the rope rail was jerking up and down. Rock had the sneaky suspicion that Beglenda was messing with him again. He turned his head to look over his shoulder and that's when he saw what the woman had been yelling about: A family of raccoons was running along the top of the rope rails toward him. A large family. A large family of large raccoons.

There were six of the darned things running his way, evenly divided among the rails (that would be three on each side for those of us who slept through math class). The coons in front were smaller, probably the children of the monsters bringing up the rear. And by "smaller," I mean that they were only maybe thirty pounds; whereas the adults running along behind were at least fifty pounders. Biggest coons Rock had ever seen.

He did some quick calculations on their total weight, adding in his, and came up with the combined gross weight of "too danged much for this rickety old bridge." His calculations proved correct as the raccoons ran right by him, not even sparing him a glance (even rudely stepping on his hands as they went by), and the bridge creaked, heaved and dipped another ten feet.

He watched the critters until they ran all the way to the other side and leapt off the railings. Unfortunately, the dip in the bridge from the extra weight didn't lessen. He was still hovering just feet above the water and figured the ropes must have stretched. *Or unraveled.* He cast a worried glance to the ancient ropes.

At that point, Rock's feet were starting to get wet from the spray of the whitecaps. He could feel the cold seeping into his supposedly waterproof boots. And of course, a breeze decided to kick up. If you can call a tree-bending, rope-bridge-swinging wind a "breeze." It was all he could do to hang on and not fall through the half-eaten, rotten boards.

Rock realized he couldn't just stand in the middle of the bridge, clinging to the ropes like a drowning man to a life preserver. Looking down at the raging river just feet below, he shook his head at that analogy. *Bad choice of words...*

Gathering his courage, chutzpah, balls, whatever you want to call it, he took a few more tentative steps and held his breath when the bridge sagged a bit more, dropping his feet completely into the tops of the whitecaps.

It was then that he started cursing Beglenda and her hair-brained, crazy adventures. The woman just never thought things through all the way, and it was always *him* who had to discover just what it was that she *hadn't* thought of. Like, for instance, the fact that the "creek" would be so swollen with the spring run-off that it would make Niagara Falls look like a leaking garden hose. Not to mention the fact that the bridge over said "creek" would be constructed of not much more than early nineteenth century twisted hemp and termite-eaten boards.

But it was too late to regret listening to the old stoned bat. He was more than halfway across by then and even though his legs were now immersed in water that shared the core temperature of an arctic iceberg, and the force of the river was twisting him and the bridge sideways, he *would* get across, or die trying. *No, scratch that last statement. I did not mean that!*

A new surge of determination went through him then and he would have raised a fist to the sky if he hadn't been clinging for dear life to the ropes. Step by agonizing step—and by agonizing, I mean really, really painful and slow—Rock forced his frozen legs to move along the bridge toward his goal. By that time, his jeans were clinging to every hair on his legs, not to mention other areas. And those "other areas" had decided to call for a formal retreat inside the relative warmth of the body, probably never to be seen again.

He wasn't sure how much time had passed. It seemed like three or four weeks, to be honest, but was probably more like fifteen minutes. But he eventually made it to the other side and hauled himself up to the bank and collapsed.

After just a few minutes, though, the adrenaline that had surged through his veins when he'd been gripping the bridge for dear life subsided and he was left with bone-shaking tremors. It didn't help that he was sure his body temperature was about the same as a frozen pork chop. The wind wasn't helping matters either.

Forcing himself to his feet, he stumbled and grabbed a tree for balance and support. He looked back across the "creek," waiting for Beglenda to cross. She was picking up all their stuff—his backpack and her purse, which was really just a stash for her weed—and Rock snorted. The bridge was still partway in the water, so she was going to get just as wet as he had, which meant all the stuff he hadn't wanted to get wet was going to. So much for precautions.

She approached the bridge then and looked down, staring at the ropes and boards as they rocked in the water. She shook her head and looked at him.

"Immnttgnnago," she yelled.

"What?" he yelled back.

Beglenda cupped her hands around her mouth. "Itztowttt immnttgnnago!"

"What?" he yelled again, cupping his hands as she had.

She shook her head again and waved as she turned back toward the path. Rock realized with horror that she was leaving. Heading back to the truck. Leaving him there, on the other side of the creek. Stranded.

He tried to calm himself by giving a mental pep talk. *It's okay. She'll get the truck, then go back to town and get help. It shouldn't be too long before they find me. They can use my cell phone to track me, right? I'll just light a fire...*

It dawned on him then as he stood shivering against the tree that Beglenda had all his survival equipment—his lighter, thermal blanket, trail mix. She also had his wallet.

And his cell phone.

After a twelve-hour stay in the wilderness, thanks to Beglenda being too stoned to give good directions to the rescuers (she finally remembered she had a map, duh), Rock racked up a several-thousand-dollar hospital bill for the treatment of hypothermia, not to mention having to replace his ruined boots. He also had the added stress of not being sure he'd ever see his man parts again.

Chapter 7 THE AGONY OF DEFEAT

Things Are All Downhill From Here

While Rock is the star in all of our stories in *Here, Hold My Beer*, suffice it to say he had plenty of help in making less-than-stellar decisions. The sheer amount of these brainless decisions really would be impossible for just one person. Ultra stupidity is a group effort. I mean, seriously, look at Congress.

To prove the point, when he was sixteen Rock's older step-brother, Giorgio, wanted to learn to snow ski to impress a girl. He talked Rock into accompanying him to the slopes and things just went, well, downhill from there.

Being teenage boys striving for total coolness, they didn't see how something called the "Bunny Run" would help their image any and decided instead to head up the ski lift to the more manly-named runs, like "Death Mountain Destiny" and "Limb Breaker Lunge." The names were slightly worrisome, but they sure weren't going to back out now, since they had spent much of their hard-earned money they'd earned working for their slave-driver dad on awesome new ski clothes, lift tickets and ski rentals. Besides, how hard could shushing down a snow-covered hill be?

Of course, there were slightly tamer-sounding runs, such as "Perilous Alpine," and those were the runs they decided to stick with. At least until they mastered the art of skiing, which they figured would take an hour or so.

Managing to survive the ski lift mount and dismount without too much embarrassment and only minimal limb flailing, the brothers decided to split up so they wouldn't draw too much attention to themselves with their efforts to learn to stay upright on three-inch-wide, six-foot long boards strapped to their feet.

Giorgio decided to head off to the south and decided to impart some pearls of wisdom to his younger stepbrother. "Just weave back and forth down the trail like those people we saw from the ski lift," he called as he pushed off with his ski poles, trying desperately to keep his feet straight while acting like he was the latest and greatest ski pro on the slopes.

Rock watched his brother for a bit, laughing as Giorgio's skis seemed to have a mind of their own when his legs suddenly separated and his arms automatically rose for balance. He looked like a pair of scissors. Rock swore he heard a "RIPPP" and wondered if Giorgio's ski pants had split. That would be so awesome.

Deciding to head over to one of the less than terrifying, yet still manly, slopes, Rock carefully turned himself around using tiny steps and cursing when the backs of his skis crossed, which nearly caused him to fall over in a most unmanly heap of down jacket and insulated ski pants.

Once he was facing in the right direction, Rock imitated Giorgio's pole pushing method and maneuvered to the top of a long, wide slope. It was perfect, not another skier in sight who might see his lack of ski-pertise and know that he was beginner, then call the authorities who would force him to stay on the Bunny Run until he could do more than take baby steps without crossing the backs of his skis and push himself with his poles. He shuddered at the possible humiliation.

Rock looked at the sign at the top of the run and decided "Mogul Madness" didn't sound too intimidating. He did wonder what the black diamond symbol meant, however. He also wondered what a "mogul" was.

Turning carefully, he pointed his skis so that he would go straight down the mountain, figuring going fast was a sure way to look cool. And a sure way to avoid looking like a bunny-run newbie.

As before when performing his amazing acts of stupi…uh, bravery, Rock found himself pausing and questioning the intelligence of his recent decision to learn to ski. But he asked himself again, "How hard can it be?" Seriously, it was just sliding downhill on two boards. If he fell, at least it would be on soft snow. It wasn't like falling out of a tree or anything.

So taking a deep frosty breath, he pushed off.

Rock soon discovered that "moguls" were huge snow walls rounded smooth on top so as to cause distance launching of skiers. He also discovered "soft snow" isn't so soft when you hit it at about two hundred miles an hour.

Giorgio's instruction to "weave back and forth" proved to be pretty much impossible, since Rock could not get his skis to cooperate, no matter how many four-letter words he used in a desperate attempt to get his thigh muscles to hold the skis, and his legs, together. So, straight down over mogul and dale he careened.

That is, until one particularly slippery mogul launched our now shrieking-like-a-little-girl-while-trying-to-remember-he-was-almost-a-man hero into the trees at the edge of the ski run.

For anyone who has ever skied and has tried tree skiing and actually survived, you're really going to appreciate this next bit. If you've never tried tree skiing, please don't. Learn from Rock's lesson. Seriously.

A trip through the trees while flying in a downward direction at a high rate of speed is terrifying, to say the least. Especially for a first-timer. Probably even for a hundredth-timer. Rock took the trip all in stride—once he stopped screaming and tried to force his testicles back down his throat. He thought he was doing a great job of dodging scratchy branches, destroying small bushes, uprooting some rather wimpy-looking trees and tossing aside an occasional mammal during his flight.

Once he miraculously made it to the bottom of the freshly-made ski trail that the resort later chose to name "Closed For Replanting," Rock collapsed, totally amazed he had survived. He sat down in the icy cold and now irritatingly soft snow, trying to assess if anything was broken and wondered how long he would have to stay in the hospital this time.

Thankfully, other than a missing ski, nothing seemed to be out of place. It shocked him that, other than his pride, nothing was really hurt. So he just sat there for a bit and enjoyed the quiet of the forest, and stared wide-eyed up at the carnage he had left in his wake.

It looked like a teenage boy-sized avalanche had come through, destroying everything in its two foot path. Of course, the path wasn't straight, since Rock had somehow managed to weave back and forth like Giorgio had advised him, probably in effort to avoid crashing into trees the size of NFL linebackers. Unfortunately, that technique was designed for a treeless ski run, one that had its snow packed down and smoothed for the more sissy skiers. When you weave back and forth through a forest at Mach II, all you really accomplish is a crooked path of destruction.

He also noted giant snowflakes wafting through the trees, gently settling here and there like a scene in a Norman Rockwell painting. A slight breeze kicked up then, sending the snowflakes up into the air once more and it was then he realized they weren't snowflakes. They were feathers. Goose down, to be exact. The breeze gusted then, causing yet another tuft of feathers to exit his ripped jacket sleeve, lifting off like dandelion fluff into the blue sky.

Rock swears to this day that he later received a statement from the US Forest Service charging him a five hundred dollar fine for chopping down trees without a permit. And he never did find his other ski.

Results: Several acres of forest destroyed; one brand-new expensive ski jacket torn; one raccoon and several squirrels needing psychotherapy; one missing rental ski.

Rocks Sink Like A…Rock

The summer after the snow skiing fiasco, Rock's stepdad, Rolando—whom everyone called Rolo—decided to buy a boat and take everyone to the lake for a week's vacation. How fun will that be? A family vacation with teenage male rivalries? Just about as much fun as plucking nose hairs.

Rock and Giorgio had both decided that waterskiing had to be much easier than snow skiing, because water was a lot softer to land in, right? I mean, if and when you fall while waterskiing, you're landing in lovely, cool water, just like sinking gently into a comforting bathtub. Too bad the guys didn't know that when plowed into at sixty miles an hour, the water is just as painfully hard as fluffy white snow is at the same speed.

Giorgio seemed to take to waterskiing quicker than Rock did, which of course was like opening the seal on an ancient tomb that released jealousy demons who swirled around Rock's head like a cloud of angry, buzzing bees.

Rock girded his loins—which is pretty darned hard with a swimsuit, let me tell you—and set himself to the task of being a better skier of water than his stupid, obnoxious stepbrother.

Rolo dragged the boys around the lake one at a time and Giorgio just got better with each pass. He managed to stay on his feet nearly every time, while Rock was still sucking water each trip around the lake…and, of course, Rock was getting angrier.

He decided to use his anger to his advantage and to really focus on staying upright. Just kidding—the truth was he was just so pissed that he couldn't see straight and so he yelled at his dad, "Go faster this time!" Rolo tried to argue that he didn't want the boy getting hurt, but Rock insisted. So Rolo punched it.

The speed actually seemed to help Rock, which really isn't surprising, considering by this time he was a speed junkie thanks to the dirt track racing he was still doing. By the second turn, he was still upright, he was starting to get the hang of it, and he was getting cockier by the second.

He released one hand from the rope and made a circular motion above his head—he wanted to go around again. Rolo obliged, since it was the first time Rock had managed to stay up for longer than four seconds.

The man gunned the boat around the next turn, which caused Rock to swing out to the side of the boat and the show-off waved at Giorgio, who was sitting behind his dad. Rock may or may not have used all four fingers when he waved.

Of course, karma is sometimes thankfully—and funnily—instant, and it was in that, uh, instant right after Rock got cocky, that he lost his balance and crashed.

It was a memorable crash. Momentous. Stunningly, spectacularly painful-looking. It was one of those waterskiing crashes in which you know a lot of lake was inhaled. And swimming trunks were lost.

After Rolo and Giorgio stopped laughing—and that took a very long, long time while Rock bobbed impatiently in the lake—they tossed him a towel to wrap himself and then headed back to shore so he could get some other shorts.

Not letting a minor lake-ingesting crash sway him, Rock insisted they get back out on the lake and keep skiing. Since it was Giorgio's turn, Rock figured he'd have a little more time to get past the nausea from swallowing lake weed and minnows, but Rolo had a better idea.

"You two can tandem ski."

Giorgio and Rock both looked at each other with the same "Huh?" expression. Rock was the one to ask the question:

"What the heck is 'tandem skiing'?"

Rolo rolled his eyes. "When you two tontos ski together, side by side. Get that other rope and tie it on."

Now, for those of you non-Italian speaking individuals, "tonto" does not, in fact, mean "Native American sidekick" or anything like that. It does, in fact, mean "dummy."

So the boys soon found themselves skiing side-by-side, with each trying to one-up the other with such risky stunts as jumping over the boat's wake. Remember, these are two boys who were waterskiing for the first time, so catching a few inches of air was a big deal.

Giorgio apparently grew a set bigger than his swimming trunks could hold and he decided to show off his newly acquired skills by crossing under Rock's rope and then back again. At that, Rock gritted his teeth so hard he thought he might have heard a "crack." When the idiot started making a move to go under his rope again, Rock had decided enough was enough. He was sick of Giorgio showing him up.

All it took was for him to lean slightly back, which lowered the rope enough to clothesline his stepbrother. What Rock hadn't planned for, though, was the fact that when Giorgio hit the rope and crashed, it was right in front of him which basically created a speed bump. Or a brick wall, rather, which is what it felt like when the two crashed.

After Rolo got the two thankfully still-clothed teenage combatants back in the boat and checked for life-threatening injuries (and while threatening to inflict injuries), he gave the two tontos a lecture (in curse-filled Italian, no less, with enough angry hand gestures to rock the boat enough to capsize it), he got a promise that they wouldn't try to kill each other. He then told them they could spend another couple of hours out on the lake.

Rock had to rethink his strategy. It was apparent that there was no way he was going to beat Giorgio at waterskiing, since the jerk seemed to have a natural talent for it. So Rock decided he would try slalom skiing. He'd seen some of the other skiers on the lake doing it, and he thought it looked pretty easy. Easier than trying to maneuver two skis, anyway.

Since Rolo'd had no idea what all he needed to outfit his new boat for skiing, the unscrupulous salesman at the outdoor store conned him into every piece of equipment they sold. There was barely enough room for the three of them in the boat thanks to that. A couple of slalom skis were included in the mix.

While Rolo dragged Giorgio around the lake a few times (and Rock was pissed to notice that Giorgio looked like he was about ready for the pro circuit), Rock worked on getting his feet attached to the slalom ski.

Finally, it was his turn. He fell over the side of the boat (on purpose, actually) and floated towards the rope in the back. As he pulled the rope to get to the end, he had a moment of satisfaction. Finally, he would get to show up that stupid Giorgio and all his show-off shenanigans. *Wait*, Rock thought to himself, *is "shenanigans" even a word? I think it is, but is it something some, like, Irish dude made up?* Rock shook his head and concentrated on getting ready for greatness.

He was bobbing in the lake waiting for Rolo to quit arguing with Giorgio about the fact that he also wanted to slalom. Rock smiled approvingly when he heard Rolo say something like "No, your brother is going to be the slalom skier," but then frowned when his stepdad added, "because he sure isn't getting any better with regular skiing."

Never mind what they think. I can do this, Rock told himself as he bobbed like a, uh, well, like a bobbin. *I'm gonna get up on my first try and then Giorgio can kiss my...well, he can suck lake water then.*

Rolo finally got tired of arguing with his son and gave him the Italian hand signal for "shut up, you idiot, I have nothing further to add and you are just ticking me off" (all Italians are familiar with it), and he started the boat.

Now because this was a slalom ski and none of them had any clue if slalom skiing was different than regular two-ski skiing, Rolo started out going kind of slow. Rock was struggling really hard to keep the tip up (that much he knew), but he was determined not to fail. He just *had* to prove that he was better than Giorgio!

As Rolo sped the boat up, Rock was having a harder time keeping the tip up out of the water to the point that the water was coming up around the ski and nearly drowning him. And he certainly wasn't even close to standing. But he was so determined (aka, stubborn as an old goat) that he refused to let go of the rope.

So determined was our young hero (okay, that's too strong of a word for Rock...maybe "main character" is better) that he even refused to let go of the rope when the ski, then his legs, and then finally his whole body submerged. So determined was he that he wouldn't even release the rope when he actually hit the bottom of the lake. Like the dirt part of the bottom. So determined (read: stubborn) was our young dude that he didn't even let go of that rope when he was dragged along the bottom of the lake, the tip of his ski plowing a trench that any farmer would be proud to plant potatoes in.

Rock finally managed to pull his legs up so he wasn't dragging the bottom and it was at this point that he realized that his archenemy, aka the stepbrother, obviously didn't bother telling Dad that Rock was no longer in sight. *Oh yeah, Giorgio's probably in the boat right now, laughing his butt off, thinking how I'm now a boat anchor and Dad's just going along wondering why the boat has no power and giving it even more gas.*

Once he freed his ski from the bottom of the lake, he was dragged back up to the surface, which was a really good thing because he was starting to get a little worried that he was going to drown.

After dodging a few trout, he made a mental note to get up early to go fishing (something Giorgio hated to do—getting up early, not fishing) so that he could catch a bunch of trout for lunch. His dad would be so happy with him then. The old guy loved fish. Rock ignored the fact that none of them could cook.

Anyway, back to our drowning stubbornly determined main character hero dude—his head finally breached the surface and he sucked in a big mouthful of air that also contained a shockingly large amount of lake water, since he was still behind a boat. But unfortunately, when he rose to the surface, his ski was behind him, and so now he was really just being dragged. This was not skiing. Not by any stretch of the imagination.

Exhaustion and the fact that he'd realized he couldn't breathe through water finally caused Rock to release the rope. He was gasping and spitting minnows and so he turned over on his back to just float for a minute to catch his breath. He couldn't wait to get back on the boat, onto any dry, hard surface that wasn't water, really, and listened for his dad to turn the boat around and come get him.

Unfortunately for our half-drowned main character, hero—oh, for Pete's sake, you get the idea—Rolo was of the generation that believed "if at first you don't succeed, then you better not wimp out, or else you look like a big baby and you'll never live it down or be able to show your face at the Italian-American Club ever again," or some sort of belief like that, and so he came around with the boat and told Rock to grab the rope and try again.

Seriously? Does that man not know that I just nearly drowned? Oh wait, he probably doesn't know, because that idiot didn't tell him I was under water. He glared at his stepbro, his suspicions confirmed when Giorgio smirked back at him. Rock knew then he was going to knock his teeth out. *Someday, anyway. Maybe not soon, since he's still about five inches taller than me...but someday I will have my revenge.*

Shaking a mental "We Will Rise!" fist at Giorgio, Rock turned his attention to the fact that Rolo was now pulling forward and the rope was tightening. This was it; his final chance to prove that he was better...well, at least that he was "as good as."

Rolo apparently decided going slow didn't work, so he gunned the boat a little harder and Rock fought to hang on to the rope as he felt himself being dragged up. He leaned back a little and pushed his legs forward, keeping the ski in front of him. They hadn't even gone twenty yards when he was up! Standing! He was slalom skiing! *Yeeeeeeeehawwwwwww!*

They toured around the lake for one pass and Rock got some confidence under his belt—uh, under his swim trunks' elastic. He relaxed a bit then and started showing off, pulling the rope so he could swing around the side of the boat where he once again gave a one-fingered wave to Giorgio, then let himself swing back around to the other side so he could get Rolo's attention, giving his stepdad a "wazzup" chin wave. He even shot Dad with a finger gun. Rolo rolled his eyes.

Apparently Rolo had enough of Rock's antics then, because he changed direction and aimed for the floating wooden ski jump. Rock saw what was coming and wavered, losing confidence for a split second, imagining flying through the air and landing belly first in the definitely not soft at all water. That split second was enough to make him bobble and lose his balance.

But it was too late; he was already just feet from the ramp when he started going down. *Oh crap, this is gonna hurt,* was the only thing he could think as his butt hit the water. Fun fact: did you know that skidding on your butt at forty miles per hour is the equivalent of an enema given via fire hose? And then he hit the ski hit the ramp.

Old wood that's constantly exposed to water has a tendency to splinter. Like long, deadly, spear-sized splinters. Rock found this out the hard way. But despite the fifty-two gallon enema and the planks of wood embedding themselves into his butt cheeks, Rock didn't let go of the rope, which is a good thing for us humor-wise, because in about point two seconds, he was off the ramp and doing this helicopter spin thing in the air. It must have been pretty spectacular, because even Giorgio stood up in the boat and pointed out his stepbrother's stunt to Rolo, whose bugged-out eyes Rock could see even from his position thirty feet up.

Alas, darned ol' Newton and his law of gravity will eventually kick in, and such was the case in Rock's short, but stunning, feat o' death. As the air decided to give up its Rock-shaped bounty and release him back to the bowels of hell, aka Navajo Lake, Rock tried to remember at least one prayer before he hit. He'd barely managed to get out, "Oh Lord" before he hit.

The momentous belly flop he'd envisioned earlier was nothing compared to the real thing. Not only did he flop on his belly, but because he was still spinning when he hit the water, he basically drilled himself into the trout-filled depths like a corkscrew into a wine bottle.

Despite the bone and belly-crunching crash that he was pretty sure at that moment left him unable to father future little Rocks, he still managed to keep his death-grip on the rope. Which, of course, meant that he was dragged through the water once again…and lost his trunks. Once again.

Results: No permanent damage and no loss of future fatherhood (as we know from reading of the misadventures of Gravel), but a major loss of pride. And swim trunks.

This is Total Bull

In every young teen boy's life there comes a time when he wants to do something dangerous. And stupid. Stupidly dangerous. No? They don't? Oh. Guess that's just Rock then.

So when Rock was sixteen, he got the sudden and inexplicable desire to be a bull rider. I know, I know. Crazy stuff. But honestly, "Urban Cowboy" had just come out and frankly, the whole country was going…country.

Back then there weren't a whole lot of rules about who could and couldn't compete in rodeo. Pretty much the only requirement for a kid was that their parents paid the entry fee and signed a release form. Rock's parents paid (well, he gave them the money, since he had a job) and signed. They were used to his less than stellar choices by then.

Now don't get me wrong. I'm not saying competing in rodeo is dumb or crazy. Actually, I love rodeo myself—from the stands, with a cold beer in hand—but it is dumb and crazy when you've never actually done anything more difficult than riding an old horse bareback and one day you decide you should hop onto the back of a several thousand pound hopping mad animal and take him for a spin around a dirt arena. Well, technically, the bull would be taking *you* for a spin, but you know what I mean.

Rock's friend, Jeremy Williams, was also feeling inspired to suffer broken bones, concussions and to get a few teeth knocked out. Rock and Jer practiced like crazy every day after school by riding a mechanical bull they built in Jer's backyard. Well, "mechanical" might be a bit of an overstatement, considering it was just a barrel tied in the air by ropes stretched between two trees and Jer's mom's clothesline. Regardless, this was the boys' training setup and they spent all afternoon nearly every day practicing.

Before long, the boys got a lot better—well, maybe not in the sense of actually staying on the bucking barrel for more than eight seconds, but they got better at pulling ropes to simulate a bucking bull and they had developed some darned impressive calluses on their hands, which they logically figured would make it easier to hold the rope on a real bull. At the very least, they both had promising careers as sailors or maybe hangmen.

An open rodeo had been announced at school where anyone with twenty bucks could join. Rock and Jer rushed right on down to the local feed store that was promoting the event and paid their money for the awesome opportunity of being crushed to death by three thousand pounds of enraged bovine. Yippee.

After spending a good chunk of his savings to buy new Wranglers, some

Dan Post boots and a black Stetson, Rock figured he was as ready as he would ever be. He looked the part anyway. Especially in the jeans, since Wranglers are stiff as boards when they're new until you wash them like a bazillion times and walking around in stiff jeans that are chafing and pinching your man parts makes you swagger like a cowboy. Just a fun fact for you.

Now Giorgio had gotten wind of Rock's rodeo dreams and had decided that he, himself, also wanted to be a rodeo cowboy. But instead of bull riding, Giorgio had chosen bronc riding. A bit less awe-inspiring than trying to stay on a twisting, bucking, rocking, steam coming out of his ears and nose bull, but it was also less dangerous. Giorgio liked to pride himself on being smarter, but Rock figured it was because his stepbrother was just afraid of getting a scar on his pretty face.

So the night of the big event, Giorgio had, suddenly and suspiciously, offered his help to get his little brother situated on the bull. While Rock squirmed, trying to get more comfortable (which was really impossible, since his legs were spread like a Chinese contortionist), Giorgio leaned in to give him the oh so needed pep talk.

"Try not to die."

What is it with my family? Rock asked himself then as he watched Giorgio tie his hand to the rope encircling the bull's body. *The best advice they ever give is "don't die." Losers.* Giorgio wrapped the rope around and around his hand, then tucked the end under the rope. Rock frowned, not sure that was legal, but hey, being tied to the bull would maybe help him stay on for eight seconds.

Whether it was legal or not, no one was around to check. Apparently no one thought a sixteen-year-old redheaded first-timer was much of a contender for the prize money and so no officials were even in sight of the chute. It was just Giorgio and Rock…and a bull named Curly Sue.

Curly Sue sure was being good while they were in the chute. He didn't even move a muscle, didn't try to slam Rock's legs in to the sides of the pen like he'd seen other bulls doing. No, he just stood there, like he was some big ol' tame puppy dog just waiting for a snack or something. Rock reached down and patted the big guy's neck.

But when the buzzer sounded and the gate opened, apparently Curly Sue had been saving every atom of energy in his body so that he could expend it all in the span of eight seconds while trying to throw the tiny, insignificant human stupidly clinging to his back into the stands. Or better yet, into the parking lot.

They whipped around, then cut back the other way. Curly Sue crow hopped straight up, then kicked his back legs out and twisted around the opposite direction. Rock was hanging on for dear life, remembering to keep his free hand in the air so that he didn't get disqualified. He just knew he was going to go the full eight seconds, though, because there was no way he could let go...the rope Giorgio had tied to his hand would have made a macramé artist weep. Or a BDSM Dom.

So around and around, up and down, around some more they went until Rock thought his neck was going to snap and the stomach that was in his throat was going to empty. His shoulder was so tight that he was pretty sure his arm was going to come right off at any moment.

Where the heck is the buzzer? Surely it's been eight seconds by now! This is ridiculous. What was I thinking? Oh yeah, I wasn't thinking. This is stupid. I'm probably going to die, or at least end up with my right arm six inches longer than my left...

It was then that Curly Sue did something Rock was pretty sure no other bull in the history of bulldom had ever done—he shot straight up on his hind legs and then plowed head first into the barricade wall between the arena and the stands. It was a crazy thing to do, almost suicidal. Rock figured then that the bull really, *really* wanted him off his back.

Apparently Rock's body thought that was a brilliant idea too, because the skin on his hand basically peeled off along with his glove so that his hand came free from the rope at about the same time that his arm really did pull out of the socket. Of course, Rock ended up doing a flip into the stands that would have garnered him at least a nine point two from gymnastics judges.

And it turns out all this was done in five seconds.

Results: Two broken ribs from crashing into the bleachers; one mild concussion; one gigantic scab on the top of his hand that forced him to write left-handed for two full weeks (his teachers swore they couldn't tell the difference); one dislocated shoulder that hurt like the devil when it was popped back in; one broken collar bone that required a sling for a full month.

You Just Can't Make This Stuff Up
Adult (chronologically, not maturely) Rock and his buds decided that they should do something more adventurous than just race cars. I mean,

seriously, anyone can race cars...a monkey in a fire suit can turn circles around a dirt track, right? (The guys themselves prove that point *cough*)

So over a case or four of beer (Elvis helped) they came up with the not so bright idea of a motorcycle demolition derby. What? You can't have a demolition derby on a motorcycle! That's crazy! Insane! Absolutely terrifying! Yep, just what they thought too and they couldn't wait to do it.

Okay, so they carefully planned the derby (just kidding, planning consisted of making sure the track was available and going to the junkyard to find motorcycles) and on the day of the race/derby/disaster, they realized that they only had a handful of guys who were willing (read: "insane enough") to get onto a motorcycle in order to purposefully crash into others. So Jimmy and Rock went up into the stands and asked any if anyone in the audience wanted to man up and participate, instead of just watching.

Now there were just enough drunks in the stands that day (it was half-price beer night) to fill all the seats of the motorcycles that Rock had bought at the junkyard for ten bucks a piece. They weren't the prettiest motorcycles, but they ran and that was all that mattered. Of course, a few had to have simple things such as handlebars and seats added to them, but after not a whole lot of money and just a little bit of shop time, they had a whole fleet of crappy looking motorcycles to use for the derby.

Once every motorcycle had a drunk and they were lined up on opposite ends of the field, the track announcer came over the loudspeaker: "Gentlemen...and ladies (since Lacy Campbell had insisted she should be allowed to ride too)...start your engines!" That was really unnecessary, since everyone had already started their engines from the second they were seated. But old man Crocker, the track owner and announcer, apparently thought the time-honored tradition was necessary.

Some girl—Rock thought she was one of Bill's recent conquests, which would mean she was probably pregnant, because all Bill had to do was ask a girl out on a date and the second the words "Do you wanna go out?" were out of his mouth, she was knocked up—walked out onto the track wearing a really short tutu looking skirt. A breeze kicked up as she held the starting flag above her head and apparently it was a panties-optional outfit, as Rock made a mental note then that she wasn't a natural blonde...*and who gets a tattoo in their armpit? Ouch!* But then she dropped her arm.

And they were off! Thirty motorcycles shot off towards each other—well, actually, twenty-eight shot off, because Bobby and Ken Whitehorse got tangled up and were already lying on the track, laughing and too drunk to stand up. But off the others went, screaming motorcycles sounding like the buzz of a million angry wasps, making the first pass at each other, trying to knock the others off their motorcycles and maybe run over a body part or two. You could practically smell the testosterone (just ask poor Lacy how it smelled out there on the track), the adrenaline, the sheer challenge that was in the air!

And before long you could see the parts that were in the air—and the bodies. Once the guys and Lacy started really going, there were parts everywhere—those handlebars that had been newly attached, brake lines, carburetors, wheels, gas tanks, helmets, shoes. And a pair of false teeth.

Rock was doing great so far—he'd managed to avoid the worst crashes and had also managed to take out four motorcycles on his own, which is, of course, the point of any demolition derby: eliminate the competition.

By the time the derby was nearly over with just a few motorcycles still operational, the place was a mess. There was carnage everywhere and it was nearly impossible to keep on the bike. Amazingly, Rock was still going, but he was having to drive over all that metal and a body or two. It was hard, but his thoughts of grandeur kept him going. *I am, after all, "Rock, Stuntman Extraordinaire." I've been doing this kind of thing since I was a kid. I'm pretty darned amazing, actually. Someone should make a show about me, like some new superhero…*

Rock's imaginings of invincibility and design of a new cape were interrupted when his front tire caught the edge of a wheel fender that was rudely lying on the track. Maybe if Rock hadn't been picturing himself standing on a hill overlooking the city while his cape flapped gently in the breeze, he might have noticed the fender and wouldn't have been going so fast. Maybe he wouldn't then have flipped his bike end over end…and maybe one more time after that…ending up flat on his back, staring up at the pretty stars in the night sky. Of course, those stars may or may not have been just those he was seeing from the impact.

Results: No winner could be declared, since by the end of the derby every competitor was lying on the track, moaning; there were twelve broken bones, a few bruised ribs, one concussion (Rock, of course, his poor head), and a few teeth missing (and not just from the false teeth). And Old Man Crocker kept all the admission fees for damages.

That Was Such A Great Idea, But How About...

Since the motorcycle derby was such a rousing success (despite hospital bills and recovery time) and a huge hit with the fans (all fifty-six of them), the guys decided they needed to expand on the idea. So after a case or three of beer (the guys were cutting back), one of them came up with the brilliant plan to host a trailer race.

Now, for those of you who haven't seen a trailer race (check YouTube, seriously...you won't be able to stop laughing), this is where you take a car or truck or whatever has a working motor, attach a trailer hitch, then pull a travel trailer, boat, or whatever you can find behind. You then pull it around the figure eight track and crash into each other, totaling a perfectly good trailer or boat, making a huge mess of the track, and an even bigger mess of the vehicle you're driving because it wasn't designed for four-wheeling over metal carnage, no matter what kind of tires, suspension or transmission the thing has.

Rock and the boys would like to take the credit for the very first trailer race, and maybe they truly did invent it, but it has sort of swept across the country. So either the idea came in a brochure packed in cases of Bud Light, or else some brain child got the idea and it spread like wildfire around Redneckville.

Regardless of how it got started, this was Rock and the boys' first time. Trailer race virgins. It was, as was all the events they staged, completely and totally planned out, right down to the day of the race when no one could remember who was in charge of advertising the event.

Word must have gotten around somehow, though, because the stands were actually full of people for a change. I mean, like nearly standing room only. Rock asked if someone had stupidly made the false claim that there was going to be free beer, but no one admitted to that. Apparently the idea of watching a bunch of semi-drunk rednecks hauling trashed out trailers and boats around a figure eight track was the Saturday night event of the year.

This time the guys didn't have to beg for participants, because every redneck and redneck wannabe in the county had begged to join the race. Junk yards for fifty miles had been bought out of old trucks, cars and any kind of trailer, RV, et cetera, they had. If a clunker could run, then a trailer hitch had been welded to it and a trailer was attached. The air at the track was filled with the smell of decades' old motor oil and mouse parts as old engines were revved in anticipation of the start of the race.

Once again, one of Bill's conquests and future baby mamas was the flag girl. At least this girl was wearing jeans so no unexpected flashes of "rug not matching the curtains" was happening. But she was wearing a hot pink tube top with no bra and when she raised the flag in the air and her top started sliding dangerously low, the guys all held their breath, hoping for a "wardrobe malfunction." But too soon, she dropped the flag.

And once again, we're off…round and round the guys went (no Lacy this time…after suffering two bruised ribs during the last derby, she'd sworn off redneck racing), swerving around the figure eight, crashing into each other. General mayhem ensued. It was awesome.

The crowd was going crazy and that fueled the guys on to go even faster, plow through even more twisted metal parts, heedless of their poor tires and oil pans and the parts that were flying dangerously into the stands. The crowd didn't mind the shrapnel coming their way; in fact, they were fighting over bumpers, hub caps and even a toilet seat that had flown out of a travel trailer.

Before long, the track was so covered in debris that you literally needed a plow on the front of your vehicle to get through it. Rock isn't even sure who "won" that night. All he knows for sure is that it took two weeks and about forty trips to the dump to clean up the mess.

Results: One hefty track fine due to the track being unusable for fifteen days; a promise of a thousand-dollar damage deposit for the next time Rock and the boys wanted to schedule an event, any event. Thankfully, no injuries this time, with the exception of Bill, who tripped over a cabinet door when he climbed out of his truck, falling and hitting his head on a boat anchor.

One Thing Leads To Another

So…the motorcycle derby was fun, but the trailer race was crazy fun, so of course, that led to the idea of the trains. (One crazy idea following another crazier idea, and then a completely insane idea is the natural progression of the male redneck brain.)

I'm sure Jack Daniels was involved in the decision and planning of the train race. I'm sure it sounded like a fantastic idea at the time, especially after a fifth or two of that amber liquid stupidity. And actually, it *was* a fantastic idea. Tons of fun for everyone (hey, that should be a slogan somewhere).

The way the train race works is you have three cars chained together. The front car is the steering and power, but has no brakes. The middle car is empty. The back car has no motor, but does have brakes. So you have a guy in the front car steering and a guy in the back car braking. With no radios or communication of any kind.

Now add twenty or so other trains and set them up on a figure eight. You can imagine the chaos.

But there was also the idea of the cruiser cars. The driver gets to steer and brake, but the passenger has the gas. The car's stereo had to work and the horn had to blow. That was a must. Rock insisted on playing The Village People's "YMCA" as loud as it would go (while doing the appropriate spelling of Y…M…C…A with their arms as they drove).

Oh, to make things more insane, the announcer could decide mid-race to change the direction of the cars.

There were so many crazy things that happened when the guys would get together and plan (and we use that term loosely): Cops and Firemen Racing (said public servants in the cruiser cars as passengers), where the cop/fireman had to jump out of the car in the infield, tackle a dummy (an actual dummy, although Rock thought long and hard about volunteering Gravel for the job), drag the dummy twenty feet across the infield, then get back in the car and strap in, then the driver would turn around and drive in the opposite direction against traffic; Poker Night, where the guys recruited professional card dealers from the nearby casinos to come and be the passengers in the cruiser cars—and the car would stop at a table in the middle of the infield, the dealer would jump out, open a fresh deck of cards, pull out the ad cards and the jokers, then deal a hand of seven-card-stud, then run and get back in the car, strap in, then the driver had to turn the car around and again go in the opposite direction; the Watermelon Race (pretty much the same thing, but passenger had to jump out, eat a big slice of watermelon); Wives and Girlfriends Night, where the driver and passenger both got out of the car, ran to the infield, picked up a dozen roses and candy, propose to their woman (or pretend to), then run back to the car and strap in and go in the opposite direction.

Now all this crazy stuff was actually done for charity. Yep, da boyz were good ol' boyz after all. They managed to get quite a bit of money for charity doing their crazy shows and races. But soon the crowds were getting bored of the same ol' same ol', so the guys decided to do something a little more exciting.

And what could be more exciting than blowing something up? Nothing I can think of.

Rock had an eighty-something Ford Tempo that was a POS (if you don't know what that term stands for, let's just go with "a crappy car"). The car had one thing after another that was wrong with it, and no matter how much time he spent fixing this, replacing that, tweaking these, adjusting those, the danged thing just would not run right. He had finally had had enough and pushed it out in the field behind his barn. Out of sight, out of mind.

But now, the talk around the second case of beer about blowing something up brought the car to mind again. Oh yeah, Rock knew exactly what they could launch into space.

That car had to die.

After a call to his good friend KC in order to procure the necessary, uh, items to blow up the car, the guys started promoting the event around the county. They figured they could make even more money than just the sale of tickets by selling raffle tickets for the chance to be the one who got to blow the thing to kingdom come.

The show was a sell-out, and the raffle tickets were gone in two days.

It was the night of the big show and the guys were happy to finally see a crowd filling the stands...except that meant there were now plenty of witnesses.

Jimmy was put in charge of the raffle and he called a little girl from the stands to draw the winning ticket. He even let the little cutie announce the winning number over the PA system. Right after she read the number, an excited shriek came from the stands and everyone turned to see who won.

It was little ol' Miss Lee, an itty bitty woman everyone knew because she was the mother of John Lee, who owned the best—and only—Chinese buffet restaurant in the county. Everyone thought John was about a hundred years old, so Miss Lee had to be older than Methuselah.

She sure didn't act like an old lady once she got down to the infield. She marched right up to Rock and pretty much pushed him out of the way (which is funny considering he weighs like two fifty and two wrens could have carried her off). Miss Lee stomped right up to the elaborate sci-fi looking board the guys had set up for the "launching pad."

There were flashing lights and buttons and knobs and levers, none of which did a single thing. But they looked cool, like a control console at a NASA flight center. The only thing that actually worked on the panel was the button that operated the detonator for the three pounds of C4 (yeah, I know, THREE???) that were packed into the Tempo. It was a big red button in the center that said "DO NOT PUSH." (Actually, it said "DONUT PUSH" because Gravel had handwritten it and his spelling isn't the best. His bottomless pit stomach might also have been involved in the process.)

The guys made a big show out of explaining to Miss Lee the intricacies of the console, which lever she had to pull, which button, et cetera. The woman gave Rock a look that said, "Yeah, right," and then leaned into his microphone and said, "Yeah, right. You so full of bull." (Of course, with her accent, it sounded like "You so fur of bur." And I'm NOT stereotyping...it really sounded like that.)

Everyone in the stands roared with laughter.

But Miss Lee is a good sport and so she followed the complicated sequence to a T and then finally pushed the big red button.

KABOOOOOOM! The explosion was far more impressive than the tree stump, that's for sure. Of course, we're talking about three times the amount of explosive here. Rock and company had made special preparations to make sure everyone was actually safe this time. I know, right? But Rock definitely didn't want a repeat of the tree stump fiasco, especially now when they were going to be dealing with flying sharp metal car parts, even if they were from a POS Ford. But even though they'd moved the car a full two hundred yards away (you can't be too safe, you know), still little bits of plastic and metal managed to rain down on the infield. Nothing too dangerous though, and since Rock and the guys had thoughtfully put a beach umbrella over the console where they stood, no one got hit. And the stands were too far away. Whew.

Results: Nothing bad this time! A lot of money was made for charity, though. But the explosion was kind of anticlimactic (not that Rock or the guys would even know what that word meant), and now they were back to scratching their heads and wondering what they could do bigger and better.

Here, Hold My Beer

And so we come to the final chapter in the life of Rock the Stuntman, before he retires and becomes Rock the Full-Time Rancher. Sometimes the decisions we make now make the decisions for the rest of our life. Dang, that was good. It should be a meme.

Bigger and better shows became the goal of the guys. They were now calling themselves bona fide stuntmen (but without the actual training a stuntman might have, and certainly without all the safety knowledge one might expect of that profession) and were pulling off such things as jumping cars with motorcycles, flying cars through fiery hoops, and the like. (Evel Knievel, you created a lot of wannabes, you do know that, right?)

But the guys were still racers at heart and so they always had to include some sort of redneck racing into every show they did.

The night of the final straw that broke Rock's back (dang near literally) was a show the guys put together called "A Night of Fire and Thunder." All the above-mentioned stunts were going to be performed, along with a school bus demolition derby, school bus figure eights (that's a trick, let me tell you), cruiser cars racing the figure eight and a poker run (remember that one?). It was a fun-packed night and the crowd was loving every minute of it.

Everything was going just perfectly. The races were a huge hit; the crowds were well lubricated with plenty of alcohol; the kids were hopped up on every sugary substance the snack bar had to offer; the guys were flying high on adrenaline. A good time was being had by all.

It was the last event—the figure eight bus race. The guys had planned on sitting that one out, since they had already scheduled themselves in every other event. So they were sitting around the infield amongst all the old school buses that had been generously donated for the event, drinking Bud Light (I swear, I did not take a kickback from Budweiser for all the mention of their product…it's just what the guys drank. Me? I prefer dark beer) and talking about the night's events.

"Went pretty good, I'd say," Rock said as he leaned back in his plastic high-backed chair and stretched his legs out while balancing his beer bottle on his belly.

"Yeah," Jimmy agreed. "I don't know why we didn't plan something big for the end though." He waved his bottle at the race going on behind him.

"This ain't much to end the show with."

Bill agreed too. "Yeah, like a jump or something, that woulda been good."

"But we already did the jumps last month," Dopey reminded them. "I think the crowd might get bored seein' the same ol' thing over and over."

"Yeah," Rock agreed, "but y'all are right, we shoulda planned a grand finale. Don't know why we didn't…"

The guys were quiet for a minute and then Rock said, "Jumpin' a school bus, now *that* woulda been somethin'."

"We already did jump a school bus!" Bill exclaimed. "Weren't you there?

Or were you too drunk to remember?" he teased. "Last month, Hector jumped his Kawasaki over that bus, lengthwise, 'member?"

Rock shook his head. "No, I'm talking about usin' the *bus* to do the jumpin'."

The guys all took exception to that and an argument ensued.

"Dad, you can't do that! It's impossible!" Gravel was the first to state his opinion and Rock started to have some hope that the alien might not be plotting his father's death after all.

Jimmy was next. "Are you crazy, boss? A bus weighs too much to get in the air. You know that."

"No way, boss. You can't get a twelve thousand pound bus in the air," Bill argued, agreeing with Jimmy.

"Much less have any hope of makin' any distance," Dopey added.

Rock's reply?

"Here, hold my beer."

He told Gravel to run to Mr. Crocker, the track owner and announcer, and tell him to make the announcement after the school bus figure eight race that there was going to be one more surprise event.

Knowing it was useless to argue with Rock, the guys all scrambled to do what they could to prepare for this absolutely insane, out of his cotton pickin' mind, what are you thinking or wait you're not, thing Rock decided to come up with at the last freaking minute.

They scrambled through the infield and searched through what was available, before Jimmy found a bus that hadn't been in the demolition derby. It was an old Blue Bird bus, in pretty decent shape, actually. They pushed the bus to the pit area so that they could perform the necessary deeds in preparing the vehicle for such an unusual and highly dangerous stunt (actually, they just charged the battery and put some gas in it). And Rock took the necessary safety precautions in order to not risk life and limb (well, he did put his fire suit and helmet back on, anyway). Yeah. Definitely not a well thought out venture.

The driver's seat on a school bus has a seat belt. Just a lap belt on the old buses. So much for the five-point safety harness that most vehicles you use to jump over any significant distance have, eh? Not to mention a roll cage, fire extinguishing system, et cetera.

Jimmy used a forklift to shove the other buses and cars and parts out of the infield and the other guys pushed the ramp they'd built for the motorcycle jumps back over into position. It was maybe, *maybe*, barely wide enough for the bus. Maybe.

Once he finally got the old thing started, Rock backed the bus up as far as it would go, all the way to the concrete wall that surrounded the track. He gunned the old motor, and then started praying for help, for safety, for wings on the bus. Honestly, he should have been praying for guidance *before* making such a stupid decision. But anyway…

The motor was a bit sputtery (no, that's not a word. Go with me here) and Rock had a brief moment of concern that he might not be able to get enough power to get the bus up the launch ramp, over the gap and onto the landing ramp. He was just about to start thinking hard about that second thought when Betty Jo McPherson, the track girl of the night and surprisingly NOT one of Bill's baby mamas, dropped the flag, signaling him to go.

Crap…well, can't back out now.

Rock slammed the gas pedal as hard as he could while he popped the clutch, then remembered he wasn't in a race car, but a big ol' metallic brick. The poor old bus made another cough and sputter before it finally took off from its position and Rock headed toward the ramp.

He was already in fifth gear and was halfway up the ramp when he realized he needed more speed, so he downshifted and punched the gas pedal again, begging the bus for more speed.

"C'mon, girl, you can do it! You gotta give me more, 'else we're both gonna crash off the end of this ramp and that ain't gonna be pretty!"

It was as if the bus heard and understood, because the ol' gal gave him everything she had and before they both knew it, they were off the end of the ramp and flying through the air!

Rock shouted in triumph! He was right! You *can* jump a school bus! He woohoo'd and yeehaw'd a few times and he might just possibly have given Bill the finger out of the bus's side window as he flew by the guys in the infield.

In just seconds, he was nearing the landing ramp. Yes, unlike when he was just a kid and hadn't thought about such things, the guys had watched enough stuntman jumps by that time to know you needed a ramp on the other side.

He could see the crowd on its feet. They were screaming and cheering and sloshing beer on one another. Rock was thrilled; this was the grand finale the crowd needed! He was already counting the proceeds they'd get from the night, figuring he'd be giving their charity a million dollar check. Okay, maybe not that much, but…a lot, anyway.

Time seemed to slow then as he approached the ramp and Rock pushed the thought aside that it was like his life passing before his eyes. *It's not like that, not at all. This is nothing like that. No, this is just such a cool thing I'm doing and I'm like a hero to these kids and they look up to me and all and the charity is gonna get a whole bunch of money and they'll think I'm a hero. Wait, no, I'm not doing this for the fame. Sure not for the fortune. We don't make no money at all. Just the opposite…these shows cost us a lot of money. But still, it's cool when people think you're…cool.*

His thoughts were interrupted then when he realized he was right over the ramp and the front end of the bus wasn't dipping. Okay, so this was going to be a butt-first landing. That's fine. No big deal.

But when the back tires hit the ramp, the bus sort of did a wheelie skid down the ramp and then the front end lurched forward and hit the pavement. Hard. Rock thought for sure his teeth had cracked with that hit. It was worse than the time Big Joe Herrera had tackled him at the homecoming game in high school and slammed him to the ground. Left a Rock-shaped dent in the field and all. He'd actually cracked two teeth that night and his jaw had been sore for weeks.

Here's a fun fact: when a bus, oh, say, is flung through the air and then comes plummeting back to earth because…gravity, the bus will perform a rocking horse maneuver. That may or may not be a technical term. Probably not. But when the front end slams down, inertia (or some other cool scientific thingy like that) takes over and sends the front of the bus back into the air (probably more likely due to the scientific thingy regarding rubber tires and shocks and springs) and so the weight is now on the back, then the front of the bus will slam back down, back up, et cetera, until said bus crashes into the concrete barrier wall.

Another fun fact: when a human body is inside a thirty-five foot, twelve-thousand pound metal tube as said metal tube crashes into a two-foot thick concrete wall with about the same force as a wrecking ball swinging with a ridiculous attention-starved pop star hanging off it, said human body does not fare well.

Results: One six-week stint in the hospital, followed by an extended vacation at a rehab convalescent center, because: 1) A crushed sternum required a metal cage to be installed to hold the rib cage apart; 2) Shattered left side of the body required titanium steel to piece it all back together; 3) Yes, yet another concussion; 4) Both hands and feet were broken. Also, let's add a lifetime of cold intolerance, leading to a need to move south, and the sad, sudden end of a stuntman's career.

sniff

But wait! That's not the end...

Epilogue THE END THAT ISN'T THE END

There comes a time in every stuntman's life when he discovers that, in fact, gravity does suck. And by that, I mean he has come to realize that his body wasn't designed to withstand repeated violent crashes into things such as cars, buses, and racetrack walls. Those crashes can be a little, um, hard on flesh and bone.

After his spectacular and horrific bus wreck, once his body had technically healed Rock found that it was harder and harder to do the simple things required of a human—things like getting out of bed, maneuvering up and down stairs, opening a beer bottle, taking a leak.

What made things even more difficult was the fact that he lived on a mountain nine thousand feet above sea level in an area prone to getting more snow than the alps in December with a wind cold enough to freeze the balls off a brass monkey (this was Rock's description, not mine).

The cold and wet combination made Rock's previously broken bones and joints ache, and on really frosty days, the titanium holding him together would absorb the cold. Imagine swallowing a popsicle whole. Think of the freezing ache that would hit your gut. So cold it almost burned. Now imagine that "burning" cold in your joints and bones. Except, unlike a popsicle that melts in bare minutes, that ache would stay with you for hours. Days. Like a brain freeze in your whole body. Yowzers.

Rock started making jokes about how he was going to "head south until they quit speaking English." He figured "south" meant warmer and warmer meant less pain. The idea was looking better and better by the following winter, when the state of Colorado had record-breaking freezes and snowfalls.

And it was entirely possible for Rock to head south, since his granddaddy died the summer before and had left Rock his house in New Mexico. While they do speak English in New Mexico (yes, it is part of the United States. You really should have paid better attention in your geography class), you at least don't need a passport to travel there. Rock didn't need anything at all to travel down south, just the price of a tank of gas. The idea was beginning to take root in his wee widdle brain.

After shoveling snow off the quarter-mile-long drive for the fifth time that day (okay, he used the snowplow attachment on his truck, but still), Rock had had enough. Enough snow. Enough cold. Enough biting wind. Enough dealing with psychotic animals. And enough living with an abusive and disloyal wife.

A few days after that extra snowy day, Rock began the process of moseying on outta Dodge. He loaded up all the crazy animals and hauled them to Dusty's big ranch. He then sold some cars. Closed up his workshop. Quit his job at the tire shop.

Then one day, he packed up some clothes and headed south. He didn't even leave a note for Skillet. He flat-out didn't want the woman to know where he was. (Before you get all up in arms about the man leaving his family, you need to know the kids were now almost full-grown. And Skillet was forever making it clear that Rock was worth more to her dead than alive. In fact, she'd taken several life insurance policies out on him. He was getting mighty tired of having to sniff his food.)

Most likely, Skillet didn't even miss the man for a month or two, not until things like the utilities got turned off because she couldn't be bothered to pay the bills. But one day she must have said, "Hey, where's my paycheck? I mean, husband?" because she packed up and followed Rock south.

Rock was perfectly happy in his granddaddy's house in sunny New Mexico. He had his favorite dogs for company and he had complete control of the television. He got a job managing a tire store and was enjoying not having anyone depending on him. No one was expecting him to put on a big show, bigger and better and crazier than the last. No one was yelling at him because he didn't make the extra three thousand that month so they could buy new furniture for the tenth time that year. There weren't any weird animals staring at him. There weren't any alien children trying to murder—or at the very least, maim—him.

His peaceful tranquility ended when Skillet knocked on the door one evening. Well, actually, she walked right in like she owned the place and within days everything was back to status quo. Rock was sniffing everything he ate. Skillet never stopped complaining and threatening him. She also still didn't understand the terms "fidelity" and "faithfulness."

And Rock had a few new wounds thanks to Gravel's help-not-help.

Rock had had enough. Again. So he took a big chunk out of his savings and bought a piece of property in a nearby town for the wife. They agreed to go their separate ways and were working on hammering out the details on a divorce. But it was taking forever, what with Skillet having the "what's mine is mine and what's yours is mine" mentality.

She found a boyfriend who moved into the house Rock bought for her (which aggravated him, but he didn't say anything). But then he met a woman who soon moved in with him.

Remember the "what's mine" attitude Skillet had? Well, that apparently went for relationships too. As soon as Rock moved the woman in, Skillet became a bit, well, super psycho. She demanded the woman leave, made threats, et cetera.

Rock tried to reason with his soon-to-be-ex, saying they were getting divorced and since she'd moved on and had a new relationship, why couldn't he? But no…apparently she thought Rock was supposed to sit alone at home and pine for her.

Not long after his new girlfriend moved in, Rock had to have yet another surgery to fix his knee that still hadn't healed completely. Skillet had known about the surgery and had even offered to take him to the hospital, which he, of course, declined. He trusted the woman about as much as he trusted a bull to behave in a field full of cows in heat.

On the day of surgery, the doctor decided they didn't need to do a full-blown knee replacement after all, but just a "roto-rootering," which translates to "you won't be laid up and incapacitated, but I still get my surgery fee." Rock was happy to know that he wouldn't have to be stuck in bed for several days after all.

The next day, Rock's new girlfriend drove him to the bank to cash his paycheck (he was starting to get the idea that she was another "all about the money" types), and while they were gone, Skillet set fire to his granddaddy's house. Yep, launched Molotov cocktails through the windows and everything. All the neighbors saw it, even got her on video in the act.

Seems that Skillet wasn't going to be ignored. She didn't want any competition (she likely was more upset that the girlfriend was the recipient of Rock's paycheck and not her), and since Rock wouldn't obey her wishes… well, she'd just punish him. Like permanently.

Since she knew Rock was having surgery the day before she'd started the fire, the police figured she thought Rock would be laid up in bed, not knowing he just got a spit shine and not a full detailing. The fire department said one of the flaming bottles landed right square in the middle of the bed in the master bedroom. Rock's room.

Apparently, Rock wasn't just being paranoid when he thought Skillet was trying to take him out all those times.

On a side note, being that the world is not a fair or just place, Skillet walked away from the arson charge without even a day in jail. This, despite several very credible eyewitnesses AND videotaped evidence. Can you say "crooked DA?"

The fire—and the loss of many things Rock held dear, most especially two of his dogs—was yet another turning point in our hero's life. Losing everything—the big house, ranch, shop and business in Colorado, then all his past mementos such as trophies and pictures—can put a new perspective on one's life. Sometimes that perspective needs a pair of binoculars. Or the Lord and Facebook. In this case, it was the latter.

Rock was lamenting his life one day (he'd booted the crazy girlfriend, who, after the fire, had gotten even loonier than Skillet, a feat he'd never thought possible) and he cried out to God something along the lines of "Is there *anyone* out there for me?" when his phone dinged that someone had liked one of his Facebook posts. That "someone" was a lady who had come into the tire store he was managing (when he was still with the soon-to-be loony gf). They'd discovered they had a lot in common and had "friended" each other on Facebook. Rock took that "ding" as a sign from above that she might just be the woman for him.

Many years later, I'm happy to report that Rock is a contented man, married to that woman whom we'll call Squirrel. He spends most of his days trying to keep Squirrel from losing all of her nuts, but he's happy to do it. And she's happy to let him.

So my friends, I will end this story (sorry, not sorry, to make it a love story at the end there) and wish you all the best for your future endeavors.

And don't forget that, should you decide not to heed the warnings at the beginning of this book, gravity does indeed suck.

Love,

Squirrel